STEP-BY-STEP

50 One-Pot Meals

STEP-BY-STEP
50 One-Pot Meals

Sarah Edmonds

Photography by Thomas Odulate

SMITHMARK

For my parents and Trevor, with love and thanks.

This edition published in 1997 by
SMITHMARK Publishers Inc.,
a divison of US Media Holdings Inc,
16 East 32nd Street, New York, NY 10016

SMITHMARK books are available for bulk purchase for sales promotion and
premium use. For details, please write or call the manager of special sales, Smithmark
Publishers Inc, 16 East 32nd Street, NY 10016; (212) 532 6600

© 1997 Anness Publishing Limited

Produced by Anness Publishing Limited
Hermes House, 88-89 Blackfriars Road, London SE1 8HA

ISBN 0-7651-9541-0

Publisher: Joanna Lorenz
Senior Editor: Linda Fraser
Designer: Joyce Chester
Photography: Thomas Odulate
Food for photography: Sarah Edmonds, assisted by Jane Wallington
Stylist: Clare Hunt

Printed and bound in Hong Kong

1 3 5 7 9 10 8 6 4 2

CONTENTS

INTRODUCTION

Mention one-pot cooking and everyone's eyes light up! Thoughts come to mind of warming comfort food, easy preparation, minimal cleaning up and wonderful pans bubbling to the brim with delicious rich stews.

All true, but the art of one-pot cooking goes much further. In this book we return to some basic cooking methods: braising, stir-frying, poaching and boiling. They may sound rather mundane but, with imagination and the amazingly wide range of ingredients available now, these techniques get a new lease on life, giving us some of the most exciting flavors we've experienced for a long time.

Browse through the soup chapter, and you'll find a recipe for every occasion. Immediately, you'll be able to see how easy these soups are to make and, with the addition of herbs, spices and unusual ingredients, how delicious and exciting they can be.

Stews and pot roasts are not necessarily the heavy dishes you may imagine: some are light and fresh, according to the season. There are delicious recipes for pastas, grains, noodles, stir-fries and sautés to provide you with endless ideas for family meals and casual entertaining. Jambalaya and Risotto are year-round hits, and Lemon Couscous Salad is perfect for summer entertaining, while the vegetarian chapter includes tasty recipes suitable for the whole family.

These recipes will become lasting favorites for quick lunches, informal evening meals or more sophisticated dinner parties.

Herbs and Spices

Use fresh herbs whenever possible; if you have to substitute dried herbs, use only about half the quantity as they have a more concentrated flavor. Dried herbs and spices should be stored in a cool, dark, dry place.

Bouquet Garni
Used to flavor soups and casseroles, a bouquet garni is usually a combination of thyme, parsley and a bay leaf, sometimes with a piece of leek or celery and black peppercorns. Buy prepared bouquets, packed in small sachets resembling tea bags, or tie your own in muslin. Remove before serving. (1)

Caraway Seeds
These small brown seeds have a slightly bitter, but warm, aniseed flavor. They are used extensively in Central European cooking in both sweet and savory dishes, such as goulash, sauerkraut, cakes and cookies. The flavor of caraway seeds goes particularly well with potatoes, onions and cheese. (2)

Chilies, Chili Powder and Crushed Chilies
There are many varieties of fresh chilies. As a general rule, the larger, fleshier chilies are milder than the small, thin, slightly wrinkled-looking ones. To reduce the heat, remove the seeds.

Chili powders come in varying strengths: make sure you read the label carefully! Most are a blend of ground chilies with other herbs and spices (often oregano and cumin seeds); others can be pure ground chili and very hot.

Crushed chilies make an excellent garnish for rice, noodle and egg dishes. (3)

Cilantro, Coriander Seeds and Ground Coriander
Quickly becoming one of the most popular flavors in cooking, cilantro has a distinct aroma and a wonderful spicy, earthy, peppery taste. It's an excellent addition to meat, fish and vegetable dishes. Add toward the end of cooking, or sprinkle over the finished dish for maximum flavor.

From the same plant, but not interchangeable with cilantro, the seeds, whole or ground, have a much spicier flavor, with a distinct hint of orange peel. Ground coriander is an essential ingredient of curry powder and it can also be found in many Moroccan-style, spicy meat and vegetable stews. (4)

Cumin and Cumin Seeds
This is another spice that goes well with meat, fish, vegetables, and cheese. It has a strong aromatic, slightly bitter flavor. Ground cumin is often paired with ground coriander. (5)

Dill Weed
The light, feathery leaves make a lovely garnish, and dill's fresh, sweet, slightly aniseed flavor is a subtle accompaniment to fish, chicken and egg dishes. It is also excellent in cream sauces. Be careful not to overpower dill's delicate flavor. Add dill towards the end of cooking for maximum flavor. (6)

Ginger (Fresh and Ground)
Used more and more in recent years, ginger's warm, sweet, spicy flavor adds a kick to any recipe, but tastes particularly good in seafood and chicken dishes. When buying fresh ginger, look for smooth plump roots. Store the unpeeled ginger, tightly wrapped, in the fridge for up to 6 weeks or so. If substituting ground ginger in a recipe, 1 teaspoon is roughly equivalent to a 1-inch piece of fresh ginger. (7)

Juniper Berries
These small, dark berries give their bittersweet pine flavor to gin. They are a perfect partner for richly flavored meats and game and can also be used in sweet dishes. Crush the berries lightly before use, to release their flavor. (8)

Kaffir Lime Leaves
These aromatic leaves add their unmistakable flavor to many Indonesian and Thai dishes. Distinctive in appearance, kaffir lime leaves are dark green, shiny, and joined in pairs, forming a figure-eight shape. The leaves freeze well so, if you find a supply, buy plenty and store them in the freezer in zip lock baggies. Add the leaves whole and remove them before eating, or finely chop the leaves and incorporate them in the dish. (9)

Lemongrass
This is a strange-looking root with a wonderful aromatic lemon flavor. Finely chop or slice the base of the root, or use the coarse stems whole and remove them before serving. If you can't find lemongrass, use a little lemon rind instead. (10)

Oregano
Oregano grows wild and has a distinctive, strong, pungent flavor. You'll recognize it in many Italian dishes, including pizzas. It is also known as wild marjoram. Marjoram is cultivated and can be used in oregano's place, though it has a more delicate flavor. (11)

Turmeric
Mildly aromatic with a slight pepper and ginger flavor, turmeric is an attractive vivid yellow color. This spice is often used to color and flavor rice and pickles and is an essential ingredient in curry powder. (12)

Cupboard Ingredients

Most of these recipes call for fresh produce, but many also make use of canned or bottled ingredients. Most of us have the basics, but here are a few suggestions for useful additions to your cupboard.

Anchovy Fillets
Canned anchovies are imported from the Mediterranean. They've been filleted and salted before being packed in oil. A little goes a long way, so use sparingly. To reduce their saltiness, soak them in a little water or milk and rinse. Add finely chopped anchovies to salads and pasta dishes or pound them to a paste and use in dressings or stir-fries. (1)

Balsamic Vinegar
This is made in the Modena region of northern Italy. It has a rich, dark color and a sweet-sour flavor. Some balsamic vinegar is aged for 15–20 years and really should be savored as a dressing. Buy a slightly cheaper, younger vinegar for cooking; it still gives an excellent flavor. In Modena, balsamic vinegar is used to dress strawberries: this traditional dish is easily prepared by sprinkling a little vinegar over sliced strawberries, then letting them stand for 30 minutes before serving. (2)

Capers
The full, unopened buds of the caper bush are picked and preserved in vinegar. They have quite a sharp flavor and need only be used in small quantities. Store in the fridge, submerged in their liquid, after opening. Capers are used extensively in Mediterranean cooking. (3)

Oils
There are many oils to choose from, all with different characteristics and uses. Some are more suited to salad dressings, others are better used for cooking or marinating foods.

Sunflower Oil
Sunflower oil (4), which is light and tasteless, is an ideal all-around oil for cooking. It can also be mixed with other highly flavored oils to dilute their strength.

Olive Oil
Extra virgin olive oil is considered the best with a maximum acidity of 1 percent. Less expensive oils, from third or fourth pressings of the olives, will usually be slightly more acidic. Use extra virgin olive oil (5) for salad dressings – drizzling it over foods for a rich olive flavor – for sauces and for dressing pasta. Keep a slightly cheaper olive oil (6) for cooking and marinating.

Sesame Oil
A strongly flavored oil, such as sesame, is an ideal cupboard ingredient (7). Just a few drops give a wonderful flavor to noodles, pasta and stir-fries and it also makes a great addition to marinades. Cook it gently or add it at the end of cooking as sesame oil burns at a low temperature.

Passata
An Italian favorite, passata is a relatively new product on the supermarket shelves, but every cupboard should have a jar! Used instead of canned tomatoes, it's made from puréed and sieved tomatoes and it makes a wonderfully smooth and flavorful base for all kinds of casseroles, soups and pasta sauces. (8)

Pine Nuts
These are the seeds collected from pine trees, such as the stone pine. The small soft oval kernel has a unique flavor that is improved by toasting before use. Pine nuts make great additions to salads, stuffings and stews and are one of the essential ingredients of pesto sauce. They have a high fat content, so don't keep them very long or they will become rancid: buy them in small quantities and use them quickly. (9)

Soy Sauce
Made from fermented soy beans, soy sauce is available in dark and light varieties. Light soy (10) should be used if only a hint of soy flavor is required and very little color. Dark soy (11) has a stronger, sweeter flavor and should be used for spicier dishes that require more robust seasoning. Remember that soy sauce is quite salty, so add extra salt sparingly.

Sun-dried Tomatoes and Sun-dried Tomato Paste
These dried tomatoes are sold either preserved in olive oil or dry; the latter need to be soaked before use. The rich, strong flavor lifts any salad, stuffing, soup or stew (12). Sun-dried tomato paste is the puréed form and adds a much fuller flavor than ordinary tomato paste. Add to sauces, casseroles and baked pasta dishes. (13)

Tabasco Sauce
This is a fiery-hot sauce, made in Louisiana from chilies. Add it to food at the table for extra spice, or use to flavor soups, stews and sauces. Add a little at a time: it's easier to add more than to take it away! (14)

Unusual Ingredients

Some of these recipes call for slightly unusual ingredients, items you may not already have in stock. It's certainly worth hunting for these; most supermarkets should stock them.

Chorizo
This spicy sausage from Spain has a coarse, meaty texture and full flavor. It's made from pork and paprika, which gives it its wonderful color. You can buy raw chorizo (1), which is similar in size to a standard sausage; you may also find ready-to-eat sausage, sliced like salami. (2)

Canned Coconut Milk (3) and Creamed Coconut (4)
Often used in Asian cooking, both versions add a creamy texture and mild coconut flavor. Most supermarkets stock blocks of creamed coconut, which is reconstituted with boiling water to the consistency you need, usually that of light cream.

Crème Fraîche
This delicious, thick cream, used extensively in French cooking, has a slightly sour taste, which is perfect in soups and casseroles, over pasta and in sauces. If you can't buy crème fraîche, use equal amounts of heavy and sour cream, mixed lightly together. (5)

Dried Porcini Mushrooms
Dried mushrooms make a tasty addition to risottos, soups and casseroles. Just a few will enrich and add a strong mushroom flavor. Dried mushrooms need to be reconstituted before use. However, don't waste the liquid they're soaked in: use it as a flavorful stock. (6)

Thai Fish Sauce
One of the main flavors of Thai cooking, Thai fish sauce is a thin, brown liquid extracted from salted, fermented fish. Use sparingly; you can always add more if you like the flavor. It is quite salty, so taste the dish before you add any extra salt. (7)

Hoisin Sauce

An essential ingredient for Asian dishes, this is a rich, dark sauce, made from soy bean paste, garlic, vinegar, spices and sugars. It gives a wonderful, sweet yet spicy flavor to poultry, meat and stir-fries and can also be used as a glaze or sauce for poultry and meat. (8)

Oyster Sauce

Although it is made from oysters, soy sauce, spices and seasonings, this sauce doesn't taste salty or fishy, but is rich and savory. Oyster sauce is a perfect partner for meat, fish and vegetables and can be used as a dipping sauce or to flavor stir-fries. (9)

Plum Sauce

A smooth, dark red-brown sauce made from plums preserved with chili, ginger, spices, vinegar and sugar. It also makes a great addition to stir-fries and marinades, or can be used as a dipping sauce. (10)

Pumpkin and Squash

You are familiar with pumpkin (11) but it's only available for a limited time each year. Most supermarkets stock butternut squash (12) and kabocha squash (13), which can be substituted for pumpkin in recipes. Pumpkin and squash are delicious on their own, but can also be added to soups and stews. They are tender and slightly nutty and go well with spices such as cumin, coriander, ginger or nutmeg.

Tahini

A pale, smooth and oily paste made from ground raw sesame seeds. It is used to flavor hummus, but can also be used to give a sesame flavor to dips, casseroles and soups. (14)

Tofu

Also known as bean curd, tofu is made from soy beans which, when puréed with water, can be strained to form a milk. A solidifying agent is added to the milk and the resulting curds are pressed. Tofu has little flavor itself but soaks up other flavors readily, so is ideal for stir-fries and desserts. Store in the fridge, covered in water. Change the water daily and it will keep for about five days. Tofu has a high protein content and is suitable for vegetarians. (15)

Water Chestnuts

White, crunchy vegetables with a juicy, sweet flavor, water chestnuts are available in cans. Drain off all the liquid and add whole or sliced. They can be eaten raw or cooked in a variety of dishes. (16)

Pasta, Noodles, Grains and Pulses

More and more types of pasta and noodles are appearing in shops and supermarkets, and there is such a wide range of pulses that the choice can be daunting. Here is a selection of ones you'll find in these recipes.

Pasta

Always choose the best you can afford. Pasta made with durum wheat and egg has a better, richer flavor. Dried pasta has improved so much that fresh is no longer necessarily better. Experiment with different brands and find one you like.

Choose a pasta suitable for the sauce: long thin noodles (1) and spaghetti (2) are better with lighter sauces, such as olive oil dressings. Thicker sauces need a pasta shape that will trap sauce in its grooves and folds. (3)

Cook pasta in plenty of boiling salted water, stirring occasionally with a fork to prevent it from sticking. Test regularly until cooked *al dente* (tender but slightly firm to the bite). Drain and return to the warm pan. Allow a little water to cling to the pasta, to prevent it from drying out and sticking together. Add the sauce and serve immediately.

Egg Noodles

Used in Asian cooking for soups and stir-fries, these noodles are rich and excellent with soy- and sesame-based sauces. Most dried egg noodles are medium or thin and are sold in compressed, flat rectangles. Simply pour boiling water over them and let stand before using. (4)

Rice Noodles

Made from rice flour and water, rice noodles (5) can be bought in a variety of widths. Authentic rice noodles are available at Chinese, Thai and other specialty food shops. The noodles need to be soaked in boiling water before being used in stir-fries and other Asian dishes.

Arborio Rice

Essential for a perfect risotto, it has shorter, rounder grains than long grain rice, with slightly translucent edges and a white, hard core. Arborio rice can absorb a lot of cooking liquid without becoming too soft, giving risotto its characteristic creamy texture but with a slight bite. (6)

Couscous

Made from semolina grains that are treated and coated with a fine wheat flour, couscous simply needs moistening, allowing the grains to swell and soften. The couscous can then be used or steamed and served piping hot. (7)

Pearl Barley

Pearl barley is the polished and refined form of the whole grain, which means it cooks more quickly. It can be added to soups and casseroles to enrich and thicken them. (8)

Chick-peas

These pale golden peas, which look a lot like hazelnuts, are an essential ingredient of hummus, a Greek dip of chick-peas, ground sesame paste, garlic and olive oil. They make a wonderful addition to soups and stews, giving a rich, nutty flavor. The dried peas (9) need lengthy soaking and cooking. Canned chick-peas make an excellent substitute. (10)

Red Kidney Beans

Probably the most well known and frequently used beans, they retain their wonderful red color when cooked. The canned variety makes an excellent addition to the cupboard. Drain and rinse well before use. (11)

Cannellini Beans

These creamy-white, slender beans have a fluffy texture and buttery flavor and are excellent in salads, soups and stews. Again, canned varieties are good. Use haricot beans if you can't buy cannellini beans. (12) and (13)

Black-eyed Peas

Attractive, pale-colored beans with a black patch where they were joined to the pod, these have a wonderful creamy flavor and add great color and texture to a dish. Try them in salads, stews and curries. (14)

Flageolets

These are pale green beans, with a fresh, subtle flavor that shouldn't be overpowered by too many spices and strong flavors. They are a variety of the bean family and are harvested before they are ripe; they are rarely available fresh here, but can be found frozen or canned. Toss flageolets in olive oil or butter and serve them as an accompaniment to lamb or chicken. Alternatively, add them to a mixed bean salad, tossed in a simple French dressing. They also make a great supper dish, cooked with plenty of onions, bacon and lemon, then seasoned well and served with crusty bread. (15)

Equipment

The right equipment makes cooking so much easier. Our guide helps you decide whether you have all you need in your kitchen, or if you need to invest in some new equipment.

Choosing Pans for One-Pot Cooking

It is important to buy the best pans you can afford; they'll definitely last a lot longer. Thin, flimsy pans burn quickly and scorch their contents and it can be difficult to maintain a constant temperature in them.

For soups, stews and pot roasts, always make sure the pan is big enough (1). Too small, and the pan may overflow or the ingredients may be packed so tightly that it could increase the cooking time. Too big, and a lot of the liquid will evaporate, causing the dish to dry out. Remember to check in the recipe whether the dish will need to go in the oven to finish cooking; if so, a flameproof casserole (2) may be more suitable than a saucepan.

Woks (3) and frying pans (4) also play a major role in one-pot cooking. Make sure you buy the right wok for your type of stove; if you cook on electric burners, you'll need one with a flat base so that it comes into contact with the heat source.

It's a matter of personal preference whether you choose non-stick frying pans or not. They certainly make life easier for some recipes, such as egg-based dishes, as they're less likely to stick. However, it is harder to get good browning on foods as the non-stick pans cannot withstand a high heat.

The one thing that really is important is a good, thick base,

to allow the heat to spread evenly and maintain a constant temperature. If your new pan comes with instructions to season it before use, it is important to follow them, as seasoning helps to prolong the life of the pan.

Roasting Pans

Choose a roasting pan (5) in which the ingredients will fit comfortably, without over-crowding. If it's too full, they'll take longer to cook; if it's too empty, your ingredients may burn. Don't forget to check that the pan will fit inside your oven!

Cutting Boards

A good-quality, thick board will last for years. Remember to keep separate boards for raw and cooked meats and fish. (6)

Knives

Using the right-sized knife for the job is very important. There are two essential knives that should be in every kitchen. A chopping knife has a heavy, wide blade and comes in a variety of sizes. Choose one with a blade that is not too large – about 7–8 inches long; this makes it easy to handle and will be ideal for chopping vegetables, meats and herbs. (7) A paring knife has a small blade and is ideal for trimming and peeling all kinds of vegetables and fruits. (8)

Measuring Cups and Spoons

Measure ingredients carefully

when following a recipe. Good measuring cups (9) and spoons (10) make this far easier.

Zester

A useful tool for cutting long, thin strips of orange, lemon or lime rind. Simply scrape over the surface – and there's no messy grater to wash up. The result is coarser than grated rind, but makes an attractive garnish. (11)

Mortar and Pestle

If you use fresh spices, a mortar and pestle is the perfect tool for crushing small amounts. (12)

Slotted Spoon

A simple utensil that is absolutely essential for one-pot cooking. When you lift browned meat from a pan, it allows the fat and juices to remain in the pan so you don't lose valuable flavor. (13)

TECHNIQUES

Browning Meat

This is very important when making stews and casseroles: the browner the meat, the richer the color and flavor of the dish.

1 Heat the pan, with a little oil, until very hot. Don't add the meat when the fat is only warm or it won't seal the outside of the meat and you'll lose a lot of the meat juices.

2 Add a few pieces of meat at a time, depending on the size of the pan, and allow it to turn a rich golden brown, turning to brown all sides. Keep the heat quite high, but be careful, as the fat will spit. Don't add the meat all at once as this reduces the heat dramatically and the meat will stew instead of sealing.

3 Remove the meat with a slotted spoon to drain off as much fat as possible, and place on paper towels. Repeat with the remaining meat.

Chopping an Onion

Chopped onions are used in many recipes and, whether they are finely or roughly chopped, the method is the same; just vary the gap between cuts to give different sized pieces.

1 Cut off the stalk end of the onion and cut it in half through the root, leaving the root intact. Remove the skin and place the halved onion, cut-side down, on the board. Make lengthwise vertical cuts into the onion, taking care not to cut right through to the root.

2 Make two or three horizontal cuts from the stalk end through to the root, but without cutting all the way through.

3 Cut the onion across from the stalk end to the root. The onion will fall away in small squares. Cut further apart for larger squares.

Using a Wok

Many one-pot recipes are suitable for cooking in a wok. It's a quick way to cook and, as long as the ingredients are prepared so they are similar in size, a good, evenly-cooked result is achieved.

1 Make sure all the ingredients are prepared and close to hand before you start, as wok cooking needs constant attention. Heat the wok for a few minutes before adding any oil.

2 When the pan is hot, add the oil and swirl it around to coat the base and sides of the wok. Allow the oil to heat for a few moments, then use a small piece of onion to test if the oil is sizzling hot.

3 Reduce the heat a little as you add the first ingredients. Stir-fry over quite high heat, but not so high that food sticks and burns. Keep the ingredients moving in the pan with a long-handled spatula or wooden spoon. If a wok dish dries out too much, don't add any more flavoring ingredients as these may unbalance the flavor; simply add a splash of water.

Peeling Tomatoes

If you have the time, peel tomatoes before adding them to sauces or stews. This avoids those unwanted, rolled-up, tough pieces of tomato skin!

1 Make a cross in each tomato with a sharp knife and place in a bowl.

2 Pour in enough boiling water to cover and let stand for 30 seconds. The skins should start to come away. Slightly unripe tomatoes may take a little longer.

3 Drain the tomatoes and peel the skin away with a sharp knife. Don't leave the tomatoes in the boiling water for too long as they tend to soften.

Preparing Fresh Ginger

Fresh ginger can be used in slices, strips or finely chopped.

1 Peel the skin off the root with a peeler or a small, sharp knife. Then cut into thin strips, using a large, sharp knife.

2 Place each piece flat on the board, cut into fine strips and use, or turn the strips around and chop them finely.

Preparing Chilies

Chilies add a distinct flavor, but remove the seeds as they are fiery-hot.

1 Always protect your hands, as chilies can irritate the skin; wear rubber gloves and never rub your eyes after handling chilies. Halve the chili lengthwise and remove and discard the seeds.

2 Slice, finely chop and use as required. Wash the knife and board thoroughly in hot, soapy water. Always wash your hands thoroughly after preparing chillies.

Preparing Garlic

Don't worry if you don't have a garlic press: try this method, which gives wonderful juicy results.

1 Break off the clove of garlic, place the flat side of a large knife on top and strike with your fist. Remove all the papery outer skin. Begin by finely chopping the clove.

2 Sprinkle a little table salt on the garlic and, using the flat side of a large knife blade, work the salt into the garlic, until it softens and releases its juices. Use as required.

Preparing Lemongrass

Use the whole stem and remove it before cooking, or chop the root.

1 Trim the end of the stem and trim off the tops, until you are left with about 4 inches.

2 Split in half lengthwise and finely chop or, if the bulb is particularly fresh, thinly slice. Use as desired.

Skinning Fish Fillets

It's easier to remove the skin before cooking than to flake the cooked fish away from it.

1 Lay the fish flat on a clean board, skin-side down, with the tail towards you. Using a sharp knife with a flexible blade, make a slit between the skin and flesh of the fillet.

2 Hold the skin with one hand. Place the knife between the skin and flesh with the edge against the skin and the blade almost parallel to it. Use a gentle sawing motion to remove the flesh, holding the skin taut underneath.

Chopping Herbs

Chop herbs just before you use them; the flavor will be much better.

1 Remove the leaves and place on a clean dry board. Use a large, sharp knife (a blunt knife will bruise, not chop, the herbs).

2 Chop the herbs, as finely or as coarsely as desired, by holding the tip of the blade on the board and rocking the handle up and down.

Grating Citrus Rind

We've all spent ages trying to get citrus rind off a grater. Try a zester: it makes life much easier!

1 Hold the edge of the zester against the side of the fruit and pull toward you. The rind comes off easily, leaving the pith behind.

2 Continue around the fruit. If you prefer smaller pieces, simply chop the rind roughly.

Thinly Slicing Vegetables

Some of the recipes call for thinly sliced vegetables; without a food processor, this could be quite tricky, but not with this technique.

1 Peel the vegetables as desired. Take a thin slice off one side, to make a base for the vegetable to stand on. This will prevent the vegetable from sliding around.

2 Stand the vegetable on its flat base and thinly slice with a sharp knife. Keep your fingers tucked underneath, using your knuckles as a guide.

Beef Noodle Soup

A steaming bowl, packed with delicious flavors and a taste of Asia.

Serves 4

INGREDIENTS

1/4 ounce dried porcini mushrooms
6 scallions
1/4 pound carrots
3/4 pound rump steak
2 tablespoons oil
1 garlic clove, crushed
1-inch piece fresh ginger,
    peeled and finely chopped
5 cups beef stock
3 tablespoons light soy sauce
1/4 cup dry sherry
3 ounces thin egg noodles
3 ounces spinach, shredded
salt and pepper

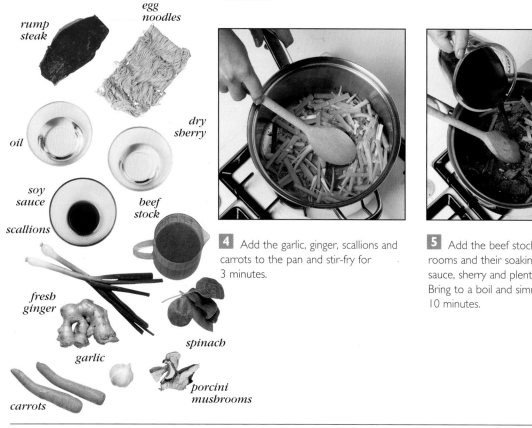

rump steak
egg noodles
oil
dry sherry
soy sauce
beef stock
scallions
fresh ginger
garlic
spinach
carrots
porcini mushrooms

1 Break the mushrooms into small pieces, place in a bowl and pour 2/3 cup boiling water over them. Let soak for 15 minutes.

2 Shred the scallions and carrots into 2-inch long, fine strips. Trim any fat off the meat and slice into thin strips.

3 Heat the oil in a large saucepan and cook the beef in batches until browned, adding a little more oil if necessary. Remove the beef with a slotted spoon and drain on paper towels.

4 Add the garlic, ginger, scallions and carrots to the pan and stir-fry for 3 minutes.

5 Add the beef stock, the mushrooms and their soaking liquid, soy sauce, sherry and plenty of seasoning. Bring to a boil and simmer, covered, for 10 minutes.

6 Break up the noodles slightly and add to the pan, with the spinach. Simmer gently for 5 minutes or until the beef is tender. Adjust the seasoning before serving.

Thai-style Chicken Soup

A fragrant blend of coconut milk, lemongrass, ginger and lime makes a delicious soup, with just a hint of chili.

Serves 4

INGREDIENTS

1 teaspoon oil
1–2 fresh red chilies,
    seeded and chopped
2 garlic cloves, crushed
1 large leek, thinly sliced
2½ cups chicken stock
1⅔ cups coconut milk
boneless, skinless chicken thighs,
    (1 pound) cut into bite-sized pieces
2 tablespoons Thai fish sauce
1 lemongrass stalk, split
1-inch piece fresh ginger, peeled and
    finely chopped
1 teaspoon sugar
4 kaffir lime leaves (optional)
¾ cup frozen peas, thawed
3 tablespoons chopped
    fresh cilantro

peas

chicken
stock

chicken
thighs

sugar

oil

fresh
cilantro

fresh
ginger

garlic

Thai fish
sauce

coconut
milk

red
chilies

lemon-
grass

leek

kaffir
lime
leaves

1 Heat the oil in a large saucepan and cook the chilies and garlic for about 2 minutes. Add the leek and cook for 2 more minutes.

2 Stir in the stock and coconut milk and bring to a boil.

3 Add the chicken, with the fish sauce, lemongrass, ginger, sugar and lime leaves, if using. Simmer, covered, for 15 minutes or until the chicken is tender, stirring occasionally.

4 Add the peas and cook for 3 more minutes. Remove the lemongrass and stir in the cilantro just before serving.

Curried Salmon Chowder

A hint of mild curry paste really enhances the flavor of this soup, without making it too spicy.

Serves 4

INGREDIENTS

¼ cup butter
½ pound onions, roughly chopped
2 teaspoons mild curry paste
⅔ cup white wine
1¼ cups heavy cream
2 ounces creamed coconut, grated
¾ pound potatoes, peeled and finely chopped
salmon fillet (1 pound), skinned and cut into bite-sized pieces
¼ cup chopped fresh flat leaf parsley
salt and pepper

onions

butter

salmon fillet

potatoes

white wine

heavy cream

curry paste

creamed coconut

flat leaf parsley

1 Melt the butter in a large saucepan, add the onions and cook over low heat for 3–4 minutes or until beginning to soften. Add the curry paste and cook for 1 more minute.

2 Add 2 cups water, the wine, cream, creamed coconut and a little seasoning. Bring to a boil, stirring until the coconut has dissolved smoothly.

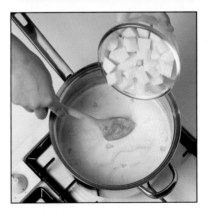

3 Add the potatoes and simmer, covered, for about 15 minutes or until they are almost tender.

4 Gently stir in the fish, being careful not to break it up too much. Simmer over very low heat for 2–3 minutes or until just tender. Add the parsley and adjust the seasoning. Serve immediately.

Mediterranean Fish Soup

This is delicious served with a rich garlic mayonnaise and plenty of crusty bread to mop up the juices. Use as many varieties of fish and shellfish as you can find.

Serves 4

INGREDIENTS

mixed fish fillets (1 pound), such as
    red mullet, monkfish, sea bass
    and/or mackerel
mixed uncooked shellfish (1 pound),
    such as mussels and shrimp
pinch of saffron strands
$\frac{1}{4}$ cup olive oil
$\frac{3}{4}$ pound onions, roughly chopped
$\frac{3}{4}$ pound fennel, halved and thinly
    sliced (about 1 small bulb)
2 teaspoons flour
1 can (14 ounces) chopped
    tomatoes, strained
3 garlic cloves, crushed
2 bay leaves
2 tablespoons chopped fresh thyme
pared rind of 1 orange
salt and cayenne pepper
garlic mayonnaise and crusty bread,
    to serve

1 Wash and skin the fish, if necessary, and cut into large chunks. Clean the shellfish and remove the heads from the shrimp.

2 Place the saffron strands in a bowl and pour $\frac{2}{3}$ cup boiling water over them. Let the saffron soak for about 20 minutes. Strain.

3 Heat the oil in a large saucepan and add the onions and fennel. Fry gently for 5 minutes, stirring occasionally, until beginning to soften.

4 Stir in the flour. Gradually blend in 3 cups water, the tomatoes, garlic, bay leaves, thyme, orange rind, saffron liquid and seasoning to taste. Bring to a boil.

mixed fish fillets

chopped tomatoes

flour

orange

bay leaves

garlic

olive oil

shrimp

onions

cayenne pepper

fennel

mussels

garlic mayonnaise

thyme

saffron

5 Reduce the heat, add the fish (not the shellfish) simmer very gently, uncovered, for about 2 minutes.

6 Add the shellfish and cook for 2–3 more minutes or until all the fish is cooked but still holding its shape. Discard any mussels that haven't opened. Adjust the seasoning. Serve in warmed bowls, with a generous spoonful of garlic mayonnaise and plenty of crusty bread.

Squash, Bacon and Swiss Cheese Soup

A lightly spiced squash soup, enriched with plenty of creamy melting cheese.

Serves 4

INGREDIENTS
butternut squash
   or pumpkin (2 pounds)
$\frac{1}{2}$ pound bacon
1 tablespoon oil
$\frac{1}{2}$ pound onions, roughly chopped
2 garlic cloves, crushed
2 teaspoons ground cumin
1 tablespoon ground coriander
10 ounces potatoes, peeled and cut
   into small chunks
$3\frac{3}{4}$ cups vegetable stock
2 teaspoons cornstarch
2 tablespoons crème fraîche
Tabasco sauce, to taste
$1\frac{1}{2}$ cups Gruyère cheese, grated
salt and pepper

ground cumin   *Tabasco sauce*   *ground coriander*

onions

butternut squash

potatoes

garlic   *oil*   *Gruyère cheese*   *cornstarch*   *bacon*   *crème fraîche*   *vegetable stock*

1 Cut the squash into large pieces. Using a sharp knife, carefully remove the skin, wasting as little as possible.

2 Scoop out the seeds and chop the squash into small chunks. Remove all the fat from the bacon and roughly chop the meat.

3 Heat the oil in a large saucepan and cook the onions and garlic for 3 minutes or until beginning to soften.

4 Add the bacon and cook for about 3 minutes. Stir in the spices and cook for 1 more minute.

5 Add the chopped squash, potatoes and stock. Bring to a boil and simmer for 15 minutes or until the squash and potatoes are tender.

6 Blend the cornstarch with 2 tablespoons water and add to the soup, with the crème fraîche. Bring to a boil and simmer, uncovered, for 3 minutes. Adjust the seasoning and add Tabasco sauce to taste. Ladle the soup into warm bowls and sprinkle on the cheese; it will just begin to melt. Serve immediately.

Caramelized Onion Soup

The onions are cooked very slowly to give this soup its rich, brown color and delicious sweet onion flavor.

Serves 4

INGREDIENTS

2 tablespoons olive oil
2 tablespoons butter
2 pounds onions, quartered
    and sliced
2 garlic cloves, crushed
1 teaspoon caraway seeds
1 tablespoon light brown sugar
1 tablespoon balsamic vinegar
2 teaspoons flour
5 cups vegetable stock
1/4 teaspoon yeast extract
grated rind and juice of 1 lemon
salt and pepper
sliced French bread and grated
    Emmenthal cheese, to serve

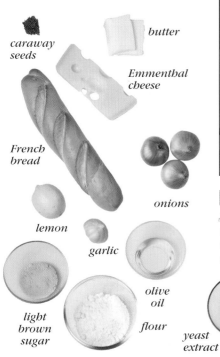

caraway seeds
butter
Emmenthal cheese
French bread
onions
lemon
garlic
olive oil
light brown sugar
flour
yeast extract
balsamic vinegar
vegetable stock

1 Heat the oil and butter in a large saucepan and add the onions, garlic, caraway seeds and sugar. Cook, covered, over medium heat, for about 20 minutes, stirring occasionally.

2 Add the balsamic vinegar and cook, uncovered, for 10 more minutes, until softened and well browned. Stir in the flour and cook over low heat for 1 minute.

3 Turn off the heat and gradually blend in the stock and yeast extract and season well. Bring to a boil, stirring, and simmer, uncovered, for about 5 minutes.

4 Stir in the grated lemon rind and 1 tablespoon of the juice and adjust the seasoning. Serve the soup topped with slices of French bread and grated Emmenthal cheese.

Spicy Peanut Soup

A thick and warming vegetable soup, flavored with chili and peanuts.

Serves 6

INGREDIENTS

2 tablespoons oil
1 large onion, finely chopped
2 garlic cloves, crushed
1 teaspoon mild chili powder
2 red bell peppers, seeded and
  finely chopped
½ pound carrots, finely chopped
½ pound potatoes, peeled and finely
  chopped
3 celery sticks, sliced
4 cups vegetable stock
6 tablespoons crunchy peanut butter
⅔ cup corn
salt and pepper
roughly chopped unsalted roasted
  peanuts, to garnish

mild chili powder

carrots

onion

corn

garlic *celery*

peanut butter

oil *red bell peppers* *potatoes* *vegetable stock* *roasted peanuts*

1 Heat the oil in a large pan and cook the onion and garlic for about 3 minutes. Add the chili powder and cook for 1 more minute.

2 Add the peppers, carrots, potatoes and celery. Stir well, then cook for 4 more minutes, stirring occasionally.

3 Stir in the stock, peanut butter and corn until combined.

4 Season well. Bring to a boil, cover and simmer for about 20 minutes or until all the vegetables are tender. Adjust the seasoning before serving, sprinkled with the chopped peanuts.

Fresh Tomato and Bean Soup

A rich chunky tomato soup, with beans and cilantro. Serve with olive ciabatta.

Serves 4

INGREDIENTS
2 pounds ripe plum tomatoes
2 tablespoons olive oil
10 ounces onions, roughly chopped
2 garlic cloves, crushed
4 cups vegetable stock
2 tablespoons sun-dried tomato paste
2 teaspoons paprika
1 tablespoon cornstarch
1 can (15 ounces) cannellini beans,
    rinsed and drained
2 tablespoons chopped fresh cilantro
salt and pepper
olive ciabatta, to serve

sun-dried tomato paste

cannellini beans

olive oil

fresh cilantro   garlic

plum tomatoes   cornstarch

paprika   vegetable stock   onions

1 First, peel the tomatoes. Using a sharp knife, make a small cross in each one and place in a bowl. Pour boiling water over them to cover and let stand for 30–60 seconds.

2 Drain the tomatoes and peel off the skins. Quarter them and then cut each piece in half again.

3 Heat the oil in a large saucepan and cook the onions and garlic for 3 minutes or until just beginning to soften.

4 Add the tomatoes to the onions, with the stock, sun-dried tomato paste and paprika. Season with a little salt and pepper. Bring to a boil and simmer for 10 minutes.

5 Mix the cornstarch to a paste with 2 tablespoons water. Stir the beans into the soup with the cornstarch paste. Cook for 5 more minutes.

6 Adjust the seasoning and stir in the chopped cilantro just before you serve with olive ciabatta.

Gazpacho

A traditional, chilled Spanish soup, perfect for a summer lunch. Make sure all the ingredients are in peak condition for the best-flavored soup.

Serves 6

INGREDIENTS
1 green bell pepper, seeded and
    roughly chopped
1 red bell pepper, seeded and
    roughly chopped
½ cucumber, roughly chopped
¾ cup onions, roughly chopped
1 fresh red chili, seeded and
    roughly chopped
1 pound ripe plum tomatoes,
    roughly chopped
3¾ cups passata or tomato juice
2 tablespoons red wine vinegar
2 tablespoons olive oil
1 tablespoon superfine sugar
salt and pepper
crushed ice, to garnish (optional)

olive oil

passata

red wine vinegar

green bell pepper

plum tomatoes

red bell pepper

superfine sugar

red chili

onions

cucumber

1 Reserve a small piece of green and red bell pepper, cucumber and onion: finely chop and set aside as a garnish.

2 Process all the remaining ingredients (except the garnish) in a blender or food processor, until smooth. You may need to do this in batches.

3 Pass the soup through a sieve into a clean glass bowl, pushing it through with a spoon, to extract as much flavor as possible.

4 Adjust the seasoning and chill. Serve sprinkled with the reserved chopped peppers, cucumber and onion. For an extra special touch, add a little crushed ice to the garnish.

Garlic, Chick-pea and Spinach Soup

This delicious, thick and creamy soup is full flavored and perfect for vegetarians.

Serves 4

INGREDIENTS

2 tablespoons olive oil
4 garlic cloves, crushed
1 onion, roughly chopped
2 teaspoons ground cumin
2 teaspoons ground coriander
5 cups vegetable stock
12 ounces potatoes, peeled and
    finely chopped
1 can (15 ounces) chick-peas,
    drained
1 tablespoon cornstarch
2/3 cup heavy cream
2 tablespoons light tahini (sesame
    seed paste)
1/2 pound spinach, shredded
cayenne pepper
salt and black pepper

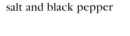
tahini   *cornstarch*

chick-peas   *cayenne pepper*   *ground coriander*

heavy cream   *garlic*   *spinach*   *potatoes*   *vegetable stock*   *ground cumin*   *olive oil*

onions

1 Heat the oil in a large saucepan and cook the garlic and onions for 5 minutes or until they are softened and golden brown.

2 Stir in the cumin and coriander and cook for another minute.

3 Pour in the stock and add the potatoes. Bring to a boil and simmer for 10 minutes. Add the drained chick-peas and simmer for 5 more minutes, or until the potatoes and chick-peas are just tender.

4 Blend the cornstarch, cream, tahini and plenty of seasoning. Stir into the soup, with the spinach. Bring to a boil, stirring, and simmer for 2 more minutes. Adjust the seasoning with salt, black pepper and cayenne pepper to taste. Serve immediately, sprinkled with a little cayenne pepper.

Cassoulet

Based on the traditional French dish, this recipe is full of delicious flavors, to make a welcoming and warming comfort-meal.

Serves 6

INGREDIENTS

boneless duck breasts (1 pound)
8 ounces thick-cut salt pork or
    unsmoked bacon
1 pound Toulouse or
    garlic sausages
3 tablespoons oil
1 pound onions, chopped
2 garlic cloves, crushed
1 can (15 ounces) cannellini beans,
    rinsed and drained
1/2 pound carrots, roughly chopped
1 can (14 ounces) chopped tomatoes
1 tablespoon tomato paste
1 bouquet garni
2 tablespoons chopped fresh thyme
2 cups chicken stock
2 cups fresh bread crumbs
salt and pepper
fresh thyme sprigs, to
    garnish (optional)
salad, to serve

garlic

garlic
sausages

chicken
stock

salt
pork

fresh bread
crumbs

cannellini
beans

tomato
paste

fresh
thyme

chopped
tomatoes

oil

duck breast

bouquet
garni

carrots

onions

1 Preheat the oven to 325°F. Cut the duck breasts and salt pork into large pieces. Twist the sausages and cut into short lengths.

2 Heat the oil in a large flameproof casserole. Cook the meat in batches, until well browned. Remove from the pan with a slotted spoon and drain on paper towels.

3 Add the onions and garlic to the pan and cook for 3–4 minutes or until beginning to soften, stirring frequently.

4 Stir in the beans, carrots, tomatoes, tomato paste, bouquet garni, thyme and seasoning. Return the meats to the pan and mix until well combined.

5 Add enough of the stock just to cover the meat and beans. (The cassoulet shouldn't be swimming in juices; if the mixture becomes too dry add a little more stock or water.) Bring to a boil. Cover tightly and cook in the oven for 1 hour.

6 Remove the cassoulet from the oven, add a little more stock or water, if necessary, and remove the bouquet garni. Sprinkle on the bread crumbs and return to the oven, uncovered, for 40 more minutes or until the meats are tender and the top crisp. Brown under the broiler, if necessary, and garnish with fresh thyme sprigs (if using). Serve with plenty of salad.

Chicken Casserole

A casserole of wonderfully tender chicken, root vegetables and lentils, finished with crème fraîche, mustard and tarragon.

Serves 4

INGREDIENTS
¾ pound onions
¾ pound trimmed leeks
¾ pound carrots
1 pound rutabaga
2 tablespoons oil
4 pieces chicken (2 pounds)
½ cup green lentils
2 cups chicken stock
1¼ cups apple juice
2 teaspoons cornstarch
3 tablespoons crème fraîche
2 teaspoons whole-grain mustard
2 tablespoons chopped fresh
   tarragon
salt and pepper
fresh tarragon sprigs, to garnish

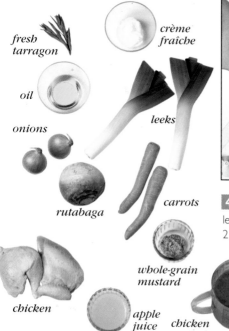

fresh tarragon
crème fraîche
oil
onions
leeks
rutabaga
carrots
chicken
whole-grain mustard
apple juice
chicken stock
green lentils
cornstarch

1 Preheat the oven to 375°F. Prepare the onions, leeks, carrots and rutabaga and roughly chop into similarly sized pieces.

2 Heat the oil in a large flameproof casserole. Season the chicken portions with salt and pepper and brown them in the hot oil until golden. Drain on paper towels.

3 Add the onions to the pan and cook for 5 minutes, until beginning to soften and color, stirring.

4 Stir in the leeks, carrots, rutabaga and lentils and stir over medium heat for 2 minutes.

5 Return the chicken to the pan. Add the stock, apple juice and seasoning. Bring to a boil and cover tightly. Cook in the oven for 50–60 minutes or until the chicken and lentils are tender.

6 Place the casserole on the stove over medium heat. Blend the cornstarch with 2 tablespoons of water and add to the casserole, with the crème fraîche, mustard and tarragon. Adjust the seasoning. Simmer gently for 2 minutes, stirring, before serving garnished with tarragon sprigs.

Citrus Beef Curry

This superbly aromatic Thai-style curry is not too hot but full of flavor. For a special meal, it goes perfectly with Thai Fried Noodles (page 64).

Serves 4

INGREDIENTS
1 pound rump steak
2 tablespoons oil
2 tablespoons medium curry paste,
   e.g. Madras
2 bay leaves
1²/₃ cups coconut milk
1¹/₄ cups beef stock
2 tablespoons lemon juice
3 tablespoons Thai fish sauce
1 tablespoon superfine sugar
¹/₄ pound baby onions, peeled but
   left whole
¹/₂ pound new potatoes, halved
²/₃ cup unsalted roasted peanuts,
   roughly chopped
¹/₄ pound green beans, halved
1 red bell pepper, seeded and
   thinly sliced
unsalted roasted peanuts,
   to garnish (optional)

rump steak

peanuts

curry paste

beef stock

baby onions *bay leaves*

red pepper

fine green beans

potatoes *oil* *Thai fish sauce* *coconut milk* *beef stock*

lemon juice *superfine sugar*

1 Trim any fat off the beef and cut into strips about 2 inches long.

2 Heat the oil in a saucepan and cook the curry paste over medium heat for 30 seconds.

3 Stir in the beef and cook for 2 minutes, until it's beginning to brown and is coated with the spices.

4 Stir in the bay leaves, coconut milk, stock, lemon juice, fish sauce and sugar. Bring to a boil, stirring.

5 Add the onions and potatoes, then bring back to a boil, reduce the heat and let simmer, uncovered, for 5 minutes.

6 Stir in the peanuts, beans and pepper and simmer for 10 more minutes or until the beef and potatoes are tender. Cook for a little longer, if necessary. Serve in shallow bowls, with a spoon and fork, to enjoy all the rich and creamy juices. Sprinkle with extra unsalted roasted peanuts, if desired.

Zesty Lamb Stew

Succulent lamb in a warm spiced gravy, with a refreshing hint of orange, is perfect served alone or with a fresh green vegetable.

Serves 6

INGREDIENTS

leg of lamb (3 pounds), boned, or
    boneless leg of lamb (2 pounds)
2 tablespoons flour
3 tablespoons oil
10 ounces onions, roughly chopped
2 garlic cloves, crushed
2 cinnamon sticks
2 red bell peppers, seeded and
    roughly chopped
1 tablespoon ground ginger
1/3 cup pearl barley
3 3/4 cups lamb or beef stock
2 tablespoons Worcestershire sauce
grated rind and juice of 1 orange
1 pound potatoes,
    roughly chopped
1 1/4 pounds rutabaga, peeled and
    roughly chopped
salt and pepper

1 Preheat the oven to 350°F. Trim any fat off the meat and cut into large cubes. Season the flour and toss the lamb in it to coat the pieces.

2 Heat the oil in a large flameproof casserole and brown the meat in batches, adding a little more oil if necessary. Remove with a slotted spoon and drain on paper towels.

3 Add the onions and garlic to the pan and cook for 3–4 minutes, until they are beginning to soften and color, stirring frequently.

oil

ground
ginger

rutabaga

cinnamon
sticks

garlic

leg of
lamb

Worcestershire sauce

potatoes

onions

beef
stock

orange

pearl
barley

flour

red bell
peppers

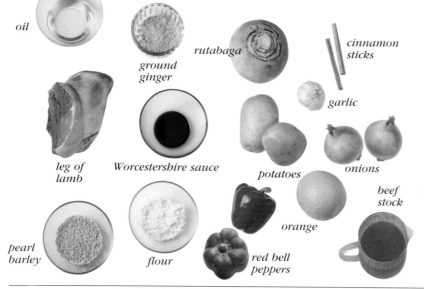

4 Stir in the cinnamon sticks, red bell peppers, ginger and pearl barley. Cook over medium heat for 2 more minutes. Add any remaining flour to the pan and cook for 1 minute.

5 Blend in the stock with the Worcestershire sauce, grated orange rind and 3 tablespoons of the juice. Season well and bring to a boil.

6 Return the meat to the pan, with the potatoes and rutabaga. Cover tightly and cook in the oven for about 1 hour and 20 minutes or until the meat and vegetables are tender. Adjust the seasoning before serving.

Fruity Cider Pork with Parsley Dumplings

Pork and fruit are a perfect combination. If you don't want to make dumplings, serve creamy mashed potatoes with the stew.

Serves 6

INGREDIENTS

scant $\frac{1}{2}$ cup pitted prunes, roughly chopped
scant $\frac{1}{4}$ cup dried apricots, roughly chopped
$1\frac{1}{4}$ cups dry cider
2 tablespoons flour
lean boneless pork ($1\frac{1}{2}$ pounds), cut into cubes
2 tablespoons oil
$\frac{3}{4}$ pound onions, roughly chopped
2 garlic cloves, crushed
6 celery sticks, roughly chopped
2 cups stock
12 juniper berries, lightly crushed
2 tablespoons chopped fresh thyme
$\frac{1}{4}$ pound self-rising flour
generous $\frac{1}{3}$ cup vegetable shortening
3 tablespoons chopped fresh parsley
1 can (15 ounces) black-eyed peas, drained
salt and pepper

1 Preheat the oven to 350°F. Place the prunes and apricots in a small bowl. Pour the cider over them and let soak for at least 20 minutes.

2 Season the flour. Toss the pork in the flour to coat; reserve any leftover flour. Heat the oil in a large flameproof casserole. Brown the meat in batches, adding a little more oil if necessary. Remove with a slotted spoon and drain on paper towels.

fresh parsley
celery
fresh thyme
onions
vegetable shortening
garlic
flour
apricots
prunes
pork
dry cider
juniper berries
black-eyed peas
oil
self-rising flour
stock

3 Add the onions, garlic and celery to the casserole and cook for 5 minutes. Add any remaining flour and cook for 1 more minute.

4 Blend in the stock, until smooth. Add the cider, with the fruit, juniper berries, thyme and plenty of seasoning. Bring to a boil, add the pork, cover tightly and cook in the oven for 50 minutes.

5 Just before the end of cooking time prepare the dumplings. Sift the flour into a bowl, then stir in the shortening and parsley. Add about 6 tablespoons of water and mix to give a smooth dough.

6 Remove the casserole from the oven, stir in the beans and adjust the seasoning. Divide the dumpling mixture into sixths, form the pieces into rounds and place on top. Return to the oven, covered, and cook for 20–25 minutes more, or until the dumplings are cooked and the pork is tender.

Fish Casserole with Lemongrass

Lemongrass gives this delicate fish casserole an aromatic flavor, perfect for a special treat.

Serves 4

INGREDIENTS

2 tablespoons butter
6 ounces onions, chopped
4 teaspoons flour
1²/₃ cups stock
²/₃ cup white wine
1-inch piece fresh ginger, peeled and
    finely chopped
2 lemongrass stalks, trimmed and
    finely chopped
1 pound new potatoes, scrubbed and
    halved if necessary
white fish fillets (1 pound), skinned
6 ounces large peeled
    cooked shrimp
10 ounces small broccoli florets
²/₃ cup heavy cream
¹/₄ cup chopped fresh chives
salt and pepper
crusty bread, to serve

butter

onions

white wine

white fish fillets

shrimp

broccoli   *lemon grass*   *heavy cream*   *fresh ginger*   *flour*   *chives*   *potatoes*   *stock*

1 Melt the butter in a large saucepan. Cook the onion for 3–4 minutes or until just tender. Stir in the flour and cook for 1 minute.

2 Stir in the stock, wine, ginger, lemongrass and potatoes. Season well and bring to a boil. Cover and cook for 15 minutes or until the potatoes are almost tender.

3 Cut the fish into large chunks. Add the fish to the pan, with the shrimp, broccoli and cream. Stir gently.

4 Simmer gently for 5 minutes, taking care not to break up the fish. Adjust the seasoning and stir in the chives. Serve with plenty of crusty bread.

Pot Roast Chicken with Lemon and Garlic

This is a rustic dish that is easy to prepare. Lardons are thick strips of bacon fat; if you can't get them, use bacon.

Serves 4

INGREDIENTS

2 tablespoons olive oil
2 tablespoons butter
1 cup smoked lardons,
   roughly chopped
8 whole garlic cloves, peeled
4 onions, quartered
2 teaspoons flour
2½ cups chicken stock
2 lemons, thickly sliced
3 tablespoons chopped fresh thyme
1 oven-ready chicken,
   (3–3½ pounds)
2 cans (14 ounces each) flageolets,
   rinsed and drained
salt and pepper
bread, to serve

smoked lardons
lemons
chicken
butter
garlic
flageolets
onions
thyme
olive oil
flour
chicken stock

1 Preheat the oven to 375°F. Heat the oil and butter in a flameproof casserole that is large enough to hold the chicken, with a little extra room around the sides. Add the lardons and cook until golden. Remove with a slotted spoon and drain on paper towels.

2 Brown the garlic and onions over high heat, until the edges are caramelized. Stir in the flour, then the stock. Return the lardons to the pan with the lemon, thyme and seasoning.

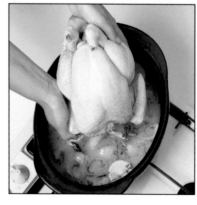

3 Bring to a boil. Then place the chicken on top, season and transfer to the oven. Cook for 1 hour, basting the chicken occasionally.

4 Baste the chicken with the juices. Stir the beans into the pan and return to the oven for 30 more minutes or until the chicken is cooked through and tender. Carve the chicken into thick slices and serve with the flageolets and plenty of bread to mop up the juices.

Pot Roast Beef with Guinness

This heart-warming, rich pot roast is ideal for a winter's supper. Beef brisket has the best flavor but this dish works equally well with arm or cross rib pot roast.

Serves 6

INGREDIENTS
2 tablespoons oil
2 pounds beef brisket
10 ounces onions,
    roughly chopped
6 celery sticks, thickly sliced
1 pound carrots, cut into large
    chunks
1½ pounds potatoes, cut into
    large chunks
2 tablespoons flour
2 cups beef stock
1¼ cups Guinness
1 bay leaf
3 tablespoons chopped fresh thyme
1 teaspoon brown sugar
2 tablespoons whole-grain mustard
1 tablespoon tomato paste
salt and pepper

beef brisket   oil

onions   celery

potatoes

thyme

flour

beef stock   bay leaf

Guinness   whole-grain
            mustard

carrots   tomato
           paste

brown
sugar

1 Preheat the oven to 350°F. Heat the oil in a large flameproof casserole and brown the meat all over, until golden. Remove from the pan and drain on paper towels.

2 Add the onions and cook for 4 minutes or until beginning to soften and turn brown, stirring constantly.

3 Add the celery, carrots and potatoes and cook over medium heat for 2–3 minutes or until they are beginning to color.

4 Add the flour and cook for 1 more minute. Blend in the stock and Guinness, until combined. Bring to a boil, stirring.

5 Stir in the bay leaf, thyme, sugar, mustard, tomato paste and plenty of seasoning. Place the meat on top, cover tightly and transfer to the oven.

6 Cook for about 2½ hours or until the vegetables and meat are tender. Adjust the seasoning and add another pinch of sugar, if necessary. To serve, remove the meat and carve into thick slices. Serve with the vegetables and plenty of Guinness gravy.

Pot Roast Glazed Lamb

The vegetables in this pot roast turn tender and caramelized with all the wonderful flavors of the meat. Spoon the juices over during cooking.

Serves 6

INGREDIENTS
12 garlic cloves
leg of lamb (2½ pounds)
    (knuckle end)
about 12 small fresh rosemary sprigs
3 tablespoons olive oil
12 shallots, peeled
2 pounds potatoes, cut into chunks
1½ pounds parsnips, cut into large
    chunks
1½ pounds carrots, cut into chunks
1¼ cups red wine
3 tablespoons clear honey
2 tablespoons dark soy sauce
2 teaspoons flour
2 cups lamb or beef stock
salt and pepper
fresh rosemary sprigs, to garnish

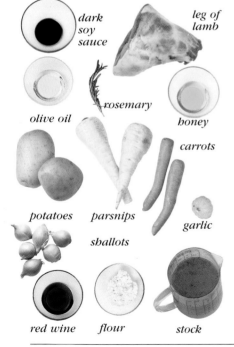

dark soy sauce
leg of lamb
olive oil
rosemary
honey
carrots
potatoes
parsnips
garlic
shallots
red wine
flour
stock

1 Preheat the oven to 375°F. Peel three of the garlic cloves and slice. Make slits all over the meat and insert slices of garlic and small sprigs of rosemary. Season well.

2 Heat the oil in a large flameproof casserole or roasting pan and add the shallots. Cook, stirring occasionally, until they begin to turn golden.

3 Add the potatoes, parsnips, carrots and remaining unpeeled cloves of garlic. Stir to coat in the oil. Season. Place the lamb on top and pour on half the red wine. Cover well, place in the oven and cook for 1 hour; baste occasionally with any fat and juices.

4 Combine the honey and soy sauce thoroughly. After the first hour of cooking, pour the honey mixture over the lamb and baste. Return to the oven, uncovered, for 1–1¼ more hours, basting the meat and vegetables occasionally.

5 Test that the meat is cooked and the vegetables are tender. Remove from the pan and let the meat rest for 10–15 minutes before carving (keep the vegetables warm).

6 Place the cooking pan on the stove, stir in the flour and cook for 1 minute. Blend in the stock and remaining wine. Bring to a boil and adjust the seasoning. Serve the meat and vegetables with plenty of juices spooned over them, garnished with rosemary.

Mediterranean Chicken

This is the perfect after-work dinner party dish: it is quick to prepare and full of sunshiny flavors.

Serves 4

INGREDIENTS

4 chicken breasts (1½ pounds total
   weight)
1 cup soft cheese with garlic
   and herbs
1 pound zucchini
2 red bell peppers, seeded
1 pound plum tomatoes
4 celery sticks
2 tablespoons olive oil
10 ounces onions, roughly chopped
3 garlic cloves, crushed
8 sun-dried tomatoes,
   roughly chopped
1 teaspoon dried oregano
2 tablespoons balsamic vinegar
1 teaspoon paprika
salt and pepper
olive ciabatta or crusty bread,
   to serve

1 Preheat the oven to 375°F. Loosen the skin of each chicken breast, without removing it, to make a pocket. Divide the cheese into fourths and push one quarter underneath the skin of each chicken breast, in an even layer.

2 Cut the zucchini and peppers into similarly sized chunky pieces. Quarter the tomatoes and slice the celery sticks.

3 Heat 2 tablespoons of the oil in a large, shallow flameproof casserole. Cook the onions and garlic for 4 minutes, until they are soft and golden, stirring frequently.

4 Add the zucchini, peppers and celery and cook for 5 more minutes.

5 Stir in the tomatoes, sun-dried tomatoes, oregano and balsamic vinegar. Season well.

6 Place the chicken on top, drizzle on a little more olive oil and season with salt and the paprika. Bake for 35–40 minutes or until the chicken is golden and cooked through. Serve with plenty of olive ciabatta or crusty bread.

olive oil

paprika

chicken

celery

sun-dried tomatoes

dried oregano

garlic

zucchini

onions

soft cheese with garlic and herbs

red bell peppers

balsamic vinegar

plum tomatoes

PASTA, GRAINS AND NOODLES

Summer Tomato Pasta

This is a deliciously light pasta dish, full of fresh flavors. Use buffalo-milk mozzarella, if you can; its flavor is so much better.

Serves 4

INGREDIENTS
2¼ cups dried penne
1 pound plum tomatoes
10 ounces mozzarella, drained
¼ cup olive oil
1 tablespoon balsamic vinegar
grated rind and juice of 1 lemon
15 fresh basil leaves, shredded
salt and black pepper
fresh basil leaves, to garnish

balsamic vinegar

basil

lemon

mozzarella

plum tomatoes

penne

olive oil

1 Cook the pasta in boiling, salted water according to the package instructions, until just tender.

2 Quarter the tomatoes and remove the seeds, then chop the flesh into cubes. Cut the mozzarella into similarly sized pieces.

3 Combine the olive oil, balsamic vinegar, grated lemon rind, 1 tablespoon of the juice and the basil. Season well. Add the tomatoes and mozzarella and let stand until the pasta is cooked.

4 Drain the pasta and toss with the tomato mixture. Serve immediately, garnished with fresh basil leaves.

Garlic and Herb Pasta

A tasty pasta dish served with plenty of fresh Parmesan cheese, this recipe makes a wonderful supper.

Serves 4

INGREDIENTS

9 ounces mixed egg and
　　spinach tagliatelle
3 garlic cloves, crushed
2 canned anchovy fillets, rinsed
　　and drained
2 tablespoons drained capers,
　　finely chopped
1 teaspoon Dijon mustard
$\frac{1}{4}$ cup olive oil
$\frac{1}{4}$ cup mixed chopped fresh chives,
　　parsley and oregano
$\frac{1}{3}$ cup pine nuts, toasted
1 tablespoon lemon juice
salt and pepper
freshly shaved Parmesan cheese,
　　to serve

oregano

capers

chives

anchovies　*olive oil*

pine nuts

Dijon mustard

tagliatelle　*garlic*

lemon juice　*Parmesan cheese*　*parsley*

1 Cook the pasta in boiling, salted water, according to the package instructions, until just tender.

2 In a mortar and pestle, pound the garlic and anchovy, until combined. Transfer to a bowl, add the capers and mustard and mix well.

3 Gradually drizzle in the olive oil, mixing until thoroughly combined. Stir in the herbs, pine nuts and lemon juice. Season well.

4 Drain the pasta and toss with the herb dressing, until well combined. Serve, sprinkled with plenty of shaved Parmesan cheese.

Jambalaya

This Cajun dish comes from the deep south. It contains a wonderful combination of rice, meat and fish, with a kick of chili. If you like *really* spicy food, add a little more chili powder to taste.

Serves 6

INGREDIENTS

boneless, skinless
    chicken thighs (1 pound)
¹/₂ pound chorizo or spicy sausages
5 celery sticks
1 red bell pepper, seeded
1 green bell pepper, seeded
2 tablespoons oil
¹/₂ pound onions,
    roughly chopped
2 garlic cloves, crushed
2 teaspoons mild chili powder
¹/₂ teaspoon ground ginger
generous 1¹/₂ cups
    long-grain white rice
3³/₄ cups
    chicken stock
6 ounces peeled cooked shrimp
salt and pepper
12 cooked shrimp in shells, with
    heads removed, to garnish

peeled shrimp
shrimp
garlic
chorizo
celery
rice
ground ginger
chili powder
chicken thighs
chicken stock
red bell pepper
green pepper

onions
oil

1 Cut the chicken and chorizo into small, bite-sized pieces. Cut the celery and peppers into thin 2-inch strips.

2 Heat the oil in a very large frying pan or large saucepan and cook the chicken until golden. Remove with a slotted spoon and drain on paper towels. Cook the chorizo for 2 minutes and drain on paper towels.

3 Add the celery and peppers and cook for 3–4 minutes, until beginning to soften and turn golden. Drain on paper towels.

4 Add a little more oil to the pan, if necessary, and cook the onions and garlic for 3 minutes. Stir in the chili powder and ginger and cook for 1 more minute.

5 Add the rice; cook for 1 minute, until it begins to look translucent. Stir in the stock, replace the chicken and bring to a boil. Cover and simmer for 12–15 minutes, stirring occasionally, until the rice is tender and the liquid absorbed. Add a little more water, if necessary during cooking.

6 Gently stir the chorizo, peppers, celery and peeled shrimp into the rice. Cook over low heat, turning the mixture over with a large spoon, until piping hot. Adjust the seasoning and serve, garnished with the whole shrimp.

Smoked Salmon Kedgeree

You could also try this recipe with grilled or poached fresh salmon: flake it and then use as for smoked salmon.

Serves 6

INGREDIENTS

scant 1½ cups long grain white rice
2 tablespoons butter
2 tablespoons olive oil
1 onion, roughly chopped
2 garlic cloves, crushed
1 red bell pepper, seeded and
   roughly chopped
¼ pound fine green beans, trimmed
   and halved
1 teaspoon mild curry paste
¼ pound peeled cooked shrimp
6 ounces smoked salmon or smoked
   salmon trimmings, roughly
   chopped
grated rind and juice of 1 lemon
¼ cup mixed chopped fresh dill and
   chives
salt and pepper
lemon wedges and fresh dill sprigs,
   to garnish
crusty bread, to serve

curry paste

green beans

garlic

butter

red bell pepper

onion

chives

lemon

dill

smoked salmon

olive oil

rice

peeled shrimp

1 Cook the rice in boiling, salted water until just tender, but still retaining a little bite (about 12 minutes). Rinse in boiling water and drain well.

2 Rinse out the pan and heat the butter and oil. Cook the onions, garlic, red bell pepper and beans for 5 minutes or until beginning to soften.

3 Add the curry paste and cook for 1 more minute. Add the shrimp and rice and stir over low heat, until both are piping hot.

4 Add the smoked salmon, with the grated lemon rind and lemon juice to taste. The salmon will begin to turn opaque. Adjust the seasoning and stir in the herbs. Serve immediately, garnished with lemon wedges and dill sprigs, with crusty bread.

Paella

Based on the classic Spanish recipe, a mixture of seafood is cooked with aromatic saffron rice.

Serves 6

INGREDIENTS
2 tablespoons olive oil
2 red bell peppers, seeded and
    roughly chopped
½ pound onions,
    roughly chopped
2 garlic cloves, crushed
¼ pound bacon, roughly chopped
scant 1¾ cups long-grain white rice
2 cups vegetable or chicken stock
1¼ cups dry white wine
pinch of saffron strands
¾ pound ripe tomatoes
1 pound mixed cooked seafood, such
    as shrimp, mussels and squid
1 cup peas, thawed
3 tablespoons chopped fresh flat
    leaf parsley
salt and pepper
whole cooked shrimp and mussels in
    their shells, to garnish

tomatoes   *onions*   *garlic*

white wine
mussels   *peas*   *parsley*

red peppers   *bacon*

shrimp   *saffron*

1 Heat 2 tablespoons oil in a paella pan. Cook the pepper for 3 minutes or until beginning to soften; remove with a slotted spoon and drain on paper towels. Add a little oil and cook the onions, garlic and bacon for 5 minutes or until the onions have softened slightly, stirring.

2 Add the rice; cook for 1 minute, until it begins to turn translucent. Stir in the saffron, stock, wine and seasoning. Boil, then simmer, covered, for 12–15 minutes. Stir occasionally.

vegetable or chicken stock   *cooked seafood*

3 Meanwhile, quarter the tomatoes and scoop out the seeds. Roughly chop the flesh.

4 When the rice is cooked and most of the liquid has been absorbed, stir the tomatoes, seafood, peas and peppers into the mixture and heat gently, stirring occasionally, for about 5 minutes or until piping hot. Stir in the parsley and adjust the seasoning before serving, garnished with the shrimp and mussels.

Smoked Bacon and Tomato Risotto

A classic risotto, with plenty of onions, smoked bacon and sun-dried tomatoes; you'll want to keep going back for more!

Serves 4

INGREDIENTS

8 sun-dried tomatoes in olive oil
10 ounces good-quality
   smoked bacon
6 tablespoons butter
2 cups onions,
   roughly chopped
2 garlic cloves, crushed
scant 1¾ cups risotto (arborio) rice
3¾ cups hot vegetable stock
1¼ cups dry white wine
⅔ cup Parmesan cheese, freshly
   grated
3 tablespoons mixed chopped fresh
   chives and flat leaf parsley
salt and pepper
lemon wedges, to serve
flat leaf parsley sprigs, to garnish

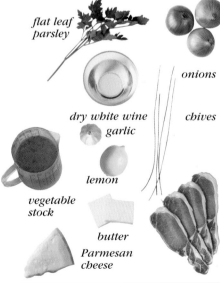

flat leaf parsley

onions

dry white wine

garlic

chives

lemon

vegetable stock

butter

Parmesan cheese

sun-dried tomatoes

smoked bacon

risotto rice

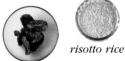

1 Drain the sun-dried tomatoes and reserve the oil. Roughly chop and set aside. Cut the smoked bacon into 1-inch strips.

2 Heat 1 tablespoon of the reserved oil in a large saucepan. Fry the bacon until well cooked and golden. Remove with a slotted spoon and drain on paper towels.

3 Add 2 tablespoons of the butter to the pan and cook the onions and garlic over medium heat for 10 minutes, until softened and golden brown.

4 Stir in the rice and cook for 1 minute, until it turns translucent. Combine the stock and wine. Add a ladleful and cook gently, until absorbed.

5 Stir in more of the stock and wine mixture as each ladleful is absorbed; this should take 20–25 minutes. The risotto will turn thick and creamy and the rice should be tender but not sticky.

6 Just before serving, stir in the bacon, sun-dried tomatoes, half the Parmesan and herbs, and the remaining butter. Adjust the seasoning (remember that the bacon could be quite salty) and serve sprinkled with the remaining Parmesan and herbs. Serve with lemon wedges, garnished with parsley.

Lemony Couscous Salad

This is a wonderful salad to pile high, and it tastes delicious served hot or cold. Add your favorite cheeses or meats to give the salad a personal touch.

Serves 6

INGREDIENTS

1²/₃ cups couscous
2¼ cups hot vegetable stock
¼ cup butter
¾ pound onions, roughly chopped
6 sun-dried tomatoes, finely chopped
5 tablespoons mixed chopped fresh chives and flat leaf parsley
¾ pound chorizo sausages, roughly chopped
1 red bell pepper, seeded and roughly chopped
1 yellow bell pepper, seeded and roughly chopped
6 ounces feta cheese, cubed
1 can (14 ounces) artichoke hearts, drained and halved
grated rind and juice of 1 lemon
¼ cup olive oil
1 teaspoon superfine sugar
salt and pepper

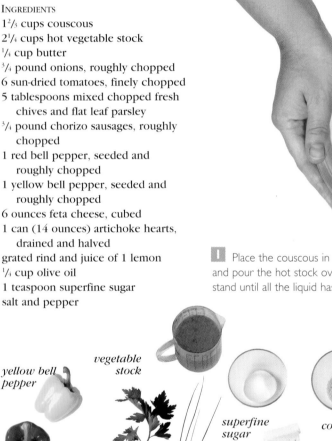

yellow bell pepper

vegetable stock

red pepper

flat leaf parsley

lemon

sun-dried tomatoes

onions

chives

superfine sugar

couscous

feta cheese

artichoke hearts

chorizo sausages

butter

olive oil

1 Place the couscous in a large bowl and pour the hot stock over it. Let stand until all the liquid has been absorbed. Gently fork the couscous to separate the grains. This can be prepared in the serving dish.

2 Heat the butter in a large frying pan and cook the onions for 5 minutes, over medium heat, until softened and golden, stirring often.

3 Add half the onions to the couscous, with the sun-dried tomatoes and 3 tablespoons of the herbs and stir until combined. Season well, transfer to a serving dish and set aside.

4 Add the chorizo and peppers to the remaining onions and cook over medium heat, until the chorizo begins to brown and the peppers have softened, 10–12 minutes. Cool the mixture slightly.

5 Toss the feta and artichokes with the chorizo mixture, season well and pile on top of the couscous. Let cool completely, if serving cold, or continue if serving warm.

6 Combine the lemon rind, 3 tablespoons of the lemon juice, the olive oil, sugar, remaining herbs and plenty of seasoning. Drizzle this dressing over the salad to serve.

Thai Fried Noodles

A staple of day-to-day Thai life, this dish is often served at Thai street stalls. It's an excellent way to make a little food go a long way. If you like Thai fish sauce, sprinkle on a little extra at the table.

Serves 4

INGREDIENTS
6 ounces rice noodles
2 tablespoons oil
2 garlic cloves, crushed
pork loin (4 ounces), finely chopped
2 canned anchovy fillets, chopped
2 tablespoons lemon juice
3 tablespoons Thai fish sauce
1 tablespoon superfine sugar
1/2 pound tofu (bean curd), cubed
2 eggs, beaten
1/4 pound peeled cooked shrimp
1/2 cup bean sprouts
1/2 cup unsalted roasted peanuts
1/4 cup chopped fresh cilantro
fresh cilantro, to garnish (optional)
dried flaked chilies and Thai fish
    sauce, to serve

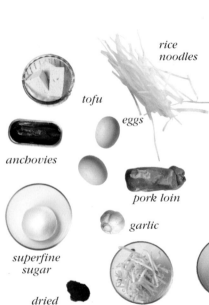

rice noodles
tofu
eggs
anchovies
pork loin
garlic
superfine sugar
dried flaked chilies
bean sprouts
Thai fish sauce
peanuts
lemon
oil
cilantro
shrimp

1 Soak the noodles in boiling water, according to the package instructions; drain well.

2 Heat the oil in a wok or large frying pan and cook the garlic until golden. Add the pork and stir-fry until cooked and golden.

3 Reduce the heat slightly and stir in the anchovies, lemon juice, fish sauce and sugar. Bring to a gentle simmer.

4 Stir in the tofu, taking care not to break it up. Fold in the noodles, until they are coated in the liquid.

5 Make a gap at the side of the pan and add the beaten eggs. Allow them to cook slightly and then stir them into the noodles.

6 Stir in the shrimp and most of the bean sprouts, peanuts and cilantro. Cook until piping hot. Serve the noodles topped with the remaining bean sprouts, peanuts and cilantro; sprinkled with a pinch of dried flaked chilies and more fish sauce, to taste. Garnish with fresh cilantro sprigs, if using.

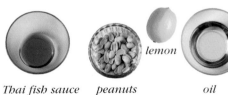

Gingered Chicken Noodles

A blend of ginger, spices and coconut milk flavors this delicious supper dish, which is made in minutes. For a real Asian touch, add a little fish sauce to taste, just before serving.

Serves 4

INGREDIENTS

boneless, skinless chicken breasts
   (³/₄ pound)
¹/₂ pound zucchini
10 ounces eggplant
2 tablespoons oil
2-inch piece fresh ginger, peeled and
   finely chopped
6 scallions, sliced
2 teaspoons Thai green curry paste
1²/₃ cups coconut milk
2 cups chicken stock
¹/₄ pound medium egg noodles
3 tablespoons chopped
   fresh cilantro
1 tablespoon lemon juice
salt and pepper
chopped fresh cilantro, to garnish

scallions
chicken breasts
cilantro
oil
chicken stock
eggplant
egg noodles
zucchini
lemon
fresh ginger
Thai green curry paste
coconut milk

1 Cut the chicken into bite-sized pieces. Halve the zucchinis lengthwise and roughly chop them. Cut the eggplant into uniform pieces.

2 Heat the oil in a large saucepan and cook the chicken until golden. Remove with a slotted spoon and drain on paper towels.

3 Add a little more oil, if necessary, and cook the ginger and scallions for 3 minutes. Add the zucchini and cook for 2–3 minutes or until beginning to turn golden. Stir in the curry paste and cook for 1 minute.

4 Add the coconut milk, stock, eggplant and chicken and simmer for 10 minutes. Add the noodles and cook for 5 minutes or until the chicken is cooked and the noodles are tender. Stir in the cilantro and lemon juice and adjust the seasoning. Serve garnished with chopped fresh cilantro.

Pork Chow Mein

A perfect speedy meal, this is flavored with sesame oil for an authentic Asian taste.

Serves 4

INGREDIENTS

6 ounces medium egg noodles
pork loin (12 ounces)
2 tablespoons sunflower oil
1 tablespoon sesame oil
2 garlic cloves, crushed
8 scallions, sliced
1 red bell pepper, seeded and
    roughly chopped
1 green bell pepper, seeded and
    roughly chopped
2 tablespoons dark soy sauce
3 tablespoons dry sherry
¾ cup bean sprouts
3 tablespoons chopped fresh flat
    leaf parsley
1 tablespoon toasted sesame seeds

red bell pepper

green bell pepper

scallions

medium egg noodles

flat leaf parsley

garlic

toasted sesame seeds

pork loin

dark soy sauce

dry sherry

sesame oil

sunflower oil

bean sprouts

1 Soak the noodles according to the package instructions. Drain well.

2 Thinly slice the pork. Heat the sunflower oil in a wok or large frying pan and cook the pork over high heat, until golden brown and cooked through.

3 Add the sesame oil to the pan, with the garlic, scallions and peppers. Cook over high heat for 3–4 minutes or until beginning to soften.

4 Reduce the heat slightly and stir in the noodles, with the soy sauce and sherry. Stir-fry for 2 minutes. Add the bean sprouts and cook for 1–2 more minutes. If the noodles begin to stick, add a splash of water. Stir in the parsley and serve sprinkled with the sesame seeds.

Spicy Chicken Stir-fry

The chicken is marinated in an aromatic blend of spices and stir-fried with crisp vegetables. If you find it too spicy, serve with a spoonful of sour cream or yogurt. It's just as delicious hot or cold.

Serves 4

INGREDIENTS
½ teaspoon each ground turmeric
   and ground ginger
1 teaspoon each salt and ground
   black pepper
2 teaspoons ground cumin
1 tablespoon ground coriander
1 tablespoon superfine sugar
boneless, skinless chicken breasts
   (1 pound)
1 bunch scallions
4 celery sticks
2 red bell peppers, seeded
1 yellow bell pepper, seeded
6 ounces zucchini
6 ounces snow peas or sugar
   snap peas
2 tablespoons sunflower oil
1 tablespoon lime juice
1 tablespoon clear honey

yellow bell pepper   *sunflower oil*   *lime*

red bell peppers   *clear honey*

celery   *zucchini*   *scallions*

ground coriander   *salt*   *sugar*

chicken breast

snow peas

ground turmeric   *ground ginger*   *ground black pepper*   *ground cumin*

1 Combine the turmeric, ginger, salt, pepper, cumin, coriander and sugar in a bowl.

2 Cut the chicken into bite-sized strips. Add to the spice mixture and stir to coat the chicken pieces thoroughly. Set aside.

3 Prepare the vegetables. Cut the scallions, celery and peppers into 2-inch long, thin strips. Cut the zucchini at a slight angle into thin rounds and trim the snow peas or sugar snap peas.

4 Heat 2 tablespoons oil in a large frying pan or wok. Stir-fry the chicken in batches until cooked through and golden brown, adding a little more oil if necessary. Remove from the pan and keep warm.

5 Add a little more oil to the pan and cook the onions, celery, peppers and zucchini over medium heat for 8–10 minutes, until beginning to soften and turn golden. Add the snow peas or sugar snap peas and cook for 2 more minutes.

6 Return the chicken to the pan, with the lime juice and honey. Cook for 2 minutes. Adjust the seasoning and serve immediately.

Beef Stir-fry with Crisp Parsnips

Wonderful crisp shreds of parsnip add extra crunchiness to this stir-fry. This is a great supper dish to share with friends.

Serves 4

INGREDIENTS
¾ pound parsnips
1 pound rump steak
1 pound trimmed leeks
2 red bell peppers, seeded
¾ pound zucchini
6 tablespoons vegetable oil
2 garlic cloves, crushed
3 tablespoons hoisin sauce
salt and pepper

vegetable oil

hoisin sauce

red bell peppers

leeks

rump steak

garlic

zucchini

parsnips

1 Peel the parsnips. Cut in half lengthwise, place the flat surface on the board and cut into thin strips. Finely shred each piece. Rinse in cold water and drain thoroughly. Dry on paper towels if necessary.

2 Cut the steak into thin strips. Split the leeks in half lengthwise and thickly slice at an angle. Roughly chop the peppers and thinly slice the zucchini.

3 Heat the oil in a wok or large frying pan. Fry the parsnips until crisp and golden. You may need to do this in batches, adding a little more oil if necessary. Remove with a slotted spoon and drain on paper towels.

4 Stir-fry the steak in the wok until golden and cooked through. You may need to do this in batches, adding more oil if necessary. Remove and drain on paper towels.

5 Stir-fry the garlic, leeks, peppers and zucchini for about 10 minutes or until golden brown and beginning to soften but still retaining a little bite. Season the mixture well.

6 Return the meat to the pan with the hoisin sauce. Stir-fry for 2–3 minutes or until piping hot. Adjust the seasoning and serve with the crisp parsnips piled on top.

Minted Lamb Stir-fry

Lamb and mint have a long-established partnership that works particularly well in this full-flavored stir-fry. Serve with plenty of crusty bread.

Serves 2

INGREDIENTS
lamb neck (10 ounces)
2 tablespoons sunflower oil
2 teaspoons sesame oil
1 onion, roughly chopped
2 garlic cloves, crushed
1 red chili, seeded and
    finely chopped
3 ounces green beans, halved
$\frac{1}{2}$ pound fresh spinach, shredded
2 tablespoons oyster sauce
2 tablespoons fish sauce
1 tablespoon lemon juice
1 teaspoon superfine sugar
3 tablespoons chopped fresh mint
salt and pepper
mint sprigs, to garnish
crusty bread, to serve

spinach

onions

lemon

garlic

lamb neck

red chili   mint

green
beans

fish sauce   sesame oil

oyster
sauce   sunflower
oil   superfine
sugar

1 Trim the lamb of any excess fat and cut into thin slices. Heat the oils in a wok or large frying pan and cook the lamb over high heat, until browned. Remove with a slotted spoon and drain on paper towels.

2 Add the onion, garlic and chili to the wok and cook for 2–3 minutes. Add the beans to the wok and stir-fry for 3 minutes.

3 Stir in the spinach with the browned meat, oyster sauce, fish sauce, lemon juice and sugar. Stir-fry for 3–4 more minutes or until the lamb is cooked through.

4 Sprinkle in the mint, adjust the seasoning and garnish with mint sprigs. Serve piping hot, with plenty of crusty bread to mop up all the juices.

Stir-fried Crispy Duck

This stir-fry would be delicious wrapped in flour tortillas or steamed Chinese pancakes, with a little extra warm plum sauce.

Serves 2

INGREDIENTS
boneless duck breast
  (³/₄ pound)
2 tablespoons flour
¹/₄ cup oil
1 bunch scallions, halved
  lengthwise and cut into
  2-inch strips
2¹/₂ cups green cabbage, finely
  shredded
1 can (8 ounces) water chestnuts,
  drained and sliced
¹/₃ cup unsalted cashews
¹/₄ pound cucumber, cut into strips
3 tablespoons plum sauce
1 tablespoon light soy sauce
salt and pepper
sliced scallions, to garnish

plum sauce   *cashews*   *oil*

water chestnuts   *flour*   *light soy sauce*

green cabbage   *scallions*

duck breast   *cucumber*

1 Trim a little of the fat from the duck and thinly slice the meat. Season the flour well and use it to coat each piece of duck.

2 Heat the oil in a wok or large frying pan and cook the duck over high heat until golden and crisp. Keep stirring to prevent the duck from sticking. Remove with a slotted spoon and drain on paper towels. You may need to do this in batches.

3 Add the scallions to the pan and cook for 2 minutes. Stir in the cabbage and cook for 5 minutes or until softened and golden.

4 Return the duck to the pan with the water chestnuts, cashews and cucumber. Stir-fry for 2 minutes. Add the plum sauce and soy sauce with plenty of seasoning, and heat for 2 minutes. Serve piping hot, garnished with sliced scallions.

Sweet-and-Sour Pork Stir-fry

This is a great idea for a quick family supper. Remember to cut the carrots into thin strips so that they cook in time.

Serves 4

INGREDIENTS

pork tenderloin (1 pound)
2 tablespoons flour
3 tablespoons oil
1 onion, roughly chopped
1 garlic clove, crushed
1 green bell pepper, seeded and sliced
³/₄ pound carrots, cut into strips
1 can (8 ounces) bamboo
    shoots, drained
1 tablespoon white wine vinegar
1 tablespoon brown sugar
2 teaspoons tomato paste
2 tablespoons light soy sauce
salt and pepper

light soy sauce   white wine vinegar   brown sugar

oil   bamboo shoots   flour

carrots   onion   green bell pepper

tomato paste

garlic   pork tenderloin

1 Thinly slice the pork. Season the flour and toss the pork in it to coat.

2 Heat the oil in a wok or large frying pan and cook the pork over medium heat for about 5 minutes, until golden and cooked through. Remove with a slotted spoon and drain on paper towels. You may need to do this in batches.

3 Add the onion and garlic to the pan and cook for 3 minutes. Stir in the pepper and carrots and stir-fry over high heat for 6–8 minutes or until beginning to soften slightly.

4 Return the meat to the pan with the bamboo shoots. Add the remaining ingredients with ½ cup water and bring to a boil. Simmer gently for 2–3 minutes or until piping hot. Adjust the seasoning, if necessary, and serve immediately.

Gingered Seafood Stir-fry

A refreshing summer supper, served with plenty of crusty bread to mop up the juices and a glass of chilled dry white wine. It would also make a great appetizer for four people.

Serves 2

INGREDIENTS
1 tablespoon sunflower oil
1 teaspoon sesame oil
1-inch piece fresh ginger, peeled and finely chopped
1 bunch scallions, sliced
1 red bell pepper, seeded and finely chopped
¼ pound small bay scallops
8 large uncooked shrimp, shelled
¼ pound squid rings
1 tablespoon lime juice
1 tablespoon light soy sauce
¼ cup coconut milk
salt and pepper
mixed lettuce leaves and crusty bread, to serve

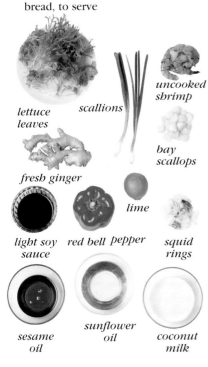

lettuce leaves *scallions* *uncooked shrimp*

fresh ginger *bay scallops*

light soy sauce *red bell pepper* *lime* *squid rings*

sesame oil *sunflower oil* *coconut milk*

1 Heat the oils in a wok or large frying pan and cook the ginger and scallions for 2–3 minutes or until golden. Stir in the red pepper and cook for 3 more minutes.

2 Add the scallops, shrimp and squid rings and cook over medium heat for about 3 minutes, until the seafood is just cooked.

3 Stir in the lime juice, soy sauce and coconut milk. Simmer, uncovered, for 2 minutes, until the juices begin to thicken slightly.

4 Season well. Arrange the lettuce leaves on serving plates and spoon on the seafood mixture with the juices. Serve with plenty of crusty bread to mop up the juices.

Vegetable Stir-fry with Eggs

A perfect family supper dish, this is very easy to prepare. Serve with plenty of crusty bread; Italian ciabatta is particularly good. Ask your butcher to cut the ham thickly in one piece.

Serves 4

INGREDIENTS
2 tablespoons olive oil
1 onion, roughly chopped
2 garlic cloves, crushed
cooked ham (6 ounces)
1/2 pound zucchini
1 red bell pepper, seeded and
    thinly sliced
1 yellow bell pepper, seeded and
    thinly sliced
2 teaspoons paprika
1 can (14 ounces) chopped tomatoes
1 tablespoon sun-dried tomato paste
    or tomato paste
4 eggs
1/4 pound Cheddar cheese, grated
salt and pepper
crusty bread, to serve

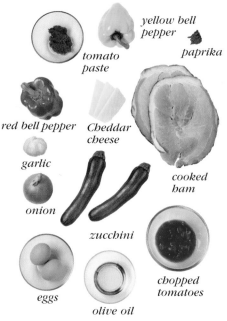

yellow bell pepper
tomato paste
paprika
red bell pepper
Cheddar cheese
garlic
cooked ham
onion
zucchini
eggs
olive oil
chopped tomatoes

1 Heat the oil in a deep frying pan and cook the onion and garlic for 4 minutes or until beginning to soften.

2 Meanwhile, cut the ham and zucchini into 2-inch batons or strips. Set the ham aside.

3 Add the zucchini and peppers to the onion and cook over medium heat for 3–4 minutes or until beginning to soften.

4 Stir in the paprika, tomatoes, sun-dried tomato paste, ham and seasoning. Bring to a boil and simmer gently for 15 minutes or until the vegetables are just tender.

5 Reduce the heat to a low setting. Make four wells in the tomato mixture, break an egg into each and season. Cook over gentle heat until the egg white begins to set.

6 Preheat the broiler to hot. Sprinkle on the cheese. Cover the pan handle with foil. Cook under the broiler for about 5 minutes, until the cheese is golden and the eggs are lightly set. Serve immediately with plenty of crusty bread.

Potatoes with Cheese

Use a firm-fleshed potato that will hold its shape when cooked. For a change, try adding chopped ham or salami between the layers.

Serves 2

INGREDIENTS
1 large onion
1 pound potatoes
2 tablespoons olive oil
2 tablespoons butter
2 garlic cloves, crushed
1 cup aged Cheddar cheese, grated
3 tablespoons chopped fresh chives
salt and pepper
chopped fresh chives, to garnish

potatoes

olive oil

butter

onion

garlic

Cheddar cheese

chives

1 Halve and thinly slice the onion. Peel and thinly slice the potatoes.

2 Heat the oil and butter in a large, heavy or non-stick frying pan. Remove from the heat and cover the base with a layer of potatoes, followed by layers of onion, garlic, cheese, chives and seasoning.

3 Continue layering, ending with cheese. Cover and cook over gentle heat for about 30 minutes or until the potatoes and onion are tender.

4 Preheat the broiler to hot. Uncover the pan, cover the pan handle with foil, and brown the top under the broiler. Serve straight from the pan, sprinkled with extra chives to garnish.

Tuna Frittata

This is the ultimate meal in a pan. For a stronger cheese flavor, why not try a creamy goat's cheese instead of the cream cheese?

Serves 2–3

INGREDIENTS
2 tablespoons butter
1 tablespoon olive oil
1 onion, finely chopped
6 ounces zucchini halved
  lengthwise and sliced
scant 1¼ cups brown-cap
  mushrooms, sliced
2 ounces asparagus tips
4 eggs, beaten
½ cup cream cheese
2 tablespoons chopped fresh thyme
1 can (7 ounces) tuna in water,
  drained and roughly flaked
¼ pound peeled cooked shrimp
salt and pepper

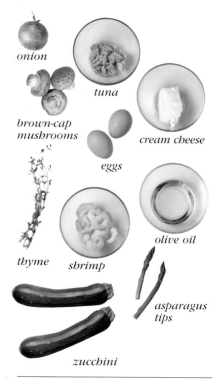

onion

tuna

brown-cap
mushrooms

cream cheese

eggs

olive oil

thyme   shrimp

asparagus
tips

zucchini

1 Heat the butter and oil in a medium-size, preferably non-stick, frying pan. Cook the onion for 3 minutes. Add the zucchini, mushrooms and asparagus and cook for 10 more minutes or until beginning to soften and brown.

2 Combine the eggs, cream cheese, thyme and plenty of seasoning until well combined.

3 Stir the tuna into the pan, being careful not to break it up too much. Add the shrimp and season well. Heat through gently. Pour on the egg mixture and cook over gentle heat for about 5 minutes, until the egg begins to set.

4 Push the egg away from the sides to allow uncooked egg to run onto the pan. Preheat the broiler to medium. Cover the pan handle with foil and place under the broiler to set and brown the surface. Serve cut in wedges.

Spicy Sausage, Caramelized Onion and Cheese Tortilla

A colorful, Spanish-style omelette, delicious served hot or cold, cut into wedges, with a tomato salad.

Serves 4-6

INGREDIENTS

1½ pounds potatoes, peeled
10 ounces onions
6 ounces chorizo or spicy sausages
5 tablespoons olive oil
4 eggs, beaten
2 tablespoons chopped fresh parsley
1 cup Cheddar
    cheese, grated
salt and pepper
fresh flat leaf parsley, to garnish

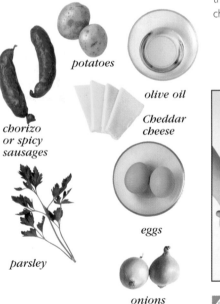

potatoes

olive oil

Cheddar cheese

chorizo or spicy sausages

eggs

parsley

onions

1 Thinly slice the potatoes. Halve and thinly slice the onions. Thinly slice the chorizo.

2 Heat 1 tablespoon oil in a non-stick frying pan, about 8 inches in diameter, and fry the sliced sausage until golden brown and cooked through. Drain on paper towels.

3 Add another 2 tablespoons of oil and fry the potatoes and onions for 2–3 minutes, turning frequently (the pan will be very full). Cover tightly and cook over gentle heat for about 30 minutes, turning occasionally, until softened and slightly golden.

4 Mix the beaten eggs in a bowl, with the parsley, cheese, sausage and plenty of seasoning. Gently stir in the potatoes and onions until coated, being careful not to break up the potatoes too much.

5 Wipe out the pan with paper towels and heat the remaining 2 tablespoons oil. Add the mixture and cook over low heat, until the egg begins to set. Use a spatula to prevent the tortilla from sticking to the sides.

6 Preheat the broiler to hot. When the base has set (after about 5 minutes), cover the pan handle with foil and place under the broiler until set and golden. Turn out, garnish with flat leaf parsley and cut into wedges to serve.

Vegetable Hot-pot with Cheese Triangles

Use a selection of your favorite vegetables, so long as the overall weight remains the same. Firm vegetables may need more cooking time.

Serves 6

INGREDIENTS
2 tablespoons oil
2 garlic cloves, crushed
1 onion, roughly chopped
1 teaspoon mild chili powder
1 pound potatoes, peeled and
    roughly chopped
1 pound celeriac, peeled and roughly
    chopped
3/4 pound carrots, roughly chopped
3/4 pound trimmed leeks,
    roughly chopped
3 cups brown-cap mushrooms,
    halved
4 teaspoons flour
2 1/2 cups vegetable stock
1 can (14 ounces) chopped tomatoes
1 tablespoon tomato paste
2 tablespoons chopped fresh thyme
1 can (14 ounces) kidney beans,
    drained and rinsed
salt and pepper

FOR THE TOPPING
1/2 cup butter
2 cups self-rising flour
1/4 cup vegetarian Cheddar cheese,
    grated
2 tablespoons snipped fresh chives
5 tablespoons milk
fresh thyme sprigs,
    to garnish (optional)

1 Preheat the oven to 350°F. Heat the oil in a large flameproof casserole and fry the garlic and onion for 5 minutes or until beginning to brown. Stir in the chili powder and cook for 1 more minute.

2 Add the potatoes, celeriac, carrots, leeks and mushrooms. Cook for 3–4 minutes. Stir in the flour and cook for 1 more minute.

3 Gradually stir in the stock with the tomatoes, tomato paste, thyme and plenty of seasoning. Bring to a boil, stirring. Cover and cook in the oven for 30 minutes.

4 Meanwhile, make the topping. Rub the butter into the flour, stir in half the cheese with the chives and plenty of seasoning. Add just enough milk to bind the mixture to a smooth dough.

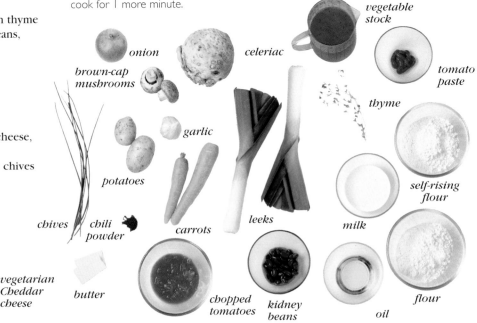

onion

brown-cap
mushrooms

celeriac

vegetable
stock

tomato
paste

thyme

garlic

self-rising
flour

potatoes

milk

chives

chili
powder

carrots

leeks

flour

vegetarian
Cheddar
cheese

butter

chopped
tomatoes

kidney
beans

oil

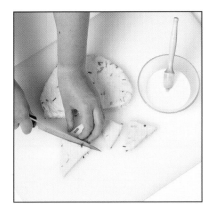

5 Roll out the dough until it is about
1 inch thick and cut into 12 triangles.
Brush with a little milk.

6 Remove the casserole from the
oven, add the beans and stir to
combine. Place the triangles on top,
overlapping them slightly, and sprinkle
with the remaining cheese. Return to
the oven, uncovered, for 20–25 minutes
or until golden brown and cooked
through. Serve, garnished with fresh
thyme sprigs, if using.

Curried Spinach and Chick-peas

Try serving this with a spoonful of plain yogurt and accompany it with naan, for a complete and very tasty meal.

Serves 6

INGREDIENTS
3 tablespoons vegetable oil
2 garlic cloves, crushed
1 onion, roughly chopped
2 tablespoons medium curry paste
1 tablespoon black mustard seeds
4 cups potatoes, cut into small cubes
1 pound frozen leaf
    spinach, thawed
1 can (14 ounces) chick-peas,
    drained
2 cups paneer cheese, cubed
1 tablespoon lime juice
salt and pepper
fresh cilantro, to garnish

lime

chick-peas

spinach

garlic

onion   *paneer cheese*   *black mustard seeds*

potatoes   *medium curry paste*   *vegetable oil*

1 Heat the oil in a large, heavy saucepan and cook the garlic and onion over medium heat for about 5 minutes or until the onion begins to soften, stirring frequently. Add the curry paste and mustard seeds and cook the mixture for 1 minute.

2 Add the potatoes, with 2 cups water. Bring to a boil and simmer gently, uncovered, for 20–25 minutes, until the potatoes are almost tender and most of the liquid has evaporated, stirring occasionally.

3 Meanwhile, place the thawed spinach in a sieve and press out as much liquid as possible. Chop roughly.

4 Stir in the spinach and chick-peas and cook for 5 more minutes or until the potatoes are tender. Add a little more water, if necessary (it should not be too wet). Stir frequently to prevent the mixture from sticking. Stir in the cheese and lime juice, adjust the seasoning and serve, garnished with fresh cilantro.

Sun-dried Tomato and Parmesan Carbonara

Ingredients for this recipe can easily be doubled to serve four. Why not try it with plenty of garlic bread and a big green salad?

Serves 2

INGREDIENTS
6 ounces tagliatelle
2 ounces sun-dried tomatoes in olive oil, drained
2 eggs, beaten
⅔ cup heavy cream
1 tablespoon whole-grain mustard
⅔ cup Parmesan cheese, freshly grated
12 fresh basil leaves, shredded
salt and pepper
fresh basil leaves, to garnish
crusty bread, to serve

1 Cook the pasta in boiling, salted water until it is just tender but still retains a little bite (*al dente*).

fresh basil

Parmesan cheese

sun-dried tomatoes

tagliatelle

whole-grain mustard

heavy cream

eggs

2 Meanwhile, cut the sun-dried tomatoes into small pieces.

3 Combine the eggs, cream and mustard with plenty of seasoning.

4 Drain the pasta and immediately return to the hot saucepan with the cream mixture, sun-dried tomatoes, Parmesan cheese and shredded fresh basil. Return to very low heat for 1 minute, stirring gently, until the mixture thickens slightly. Adjust the seasoning and serve immediately, garnished with basil leaves. Serve with plenty of crusty bread.

Asian Fried Rice

This is a great way to use leftover cooked rice.
Make sure the rice is very cold before attempting
to fry it: warm rice will become soggy.

Serves 4-6

INGREDIENTS

5 tablespoons oil
¼ pound shallots, halved and
   thinly sliced
3 garlic cloves, crushed
1 red chili, seeded and
   finely chopped
6 scallions, finely chopped
1 red bell pepper, seeded and
   finely chopped
½ pound white cabbage,
   finely shredded
6 ounces cucumber,
   finely chopped
½ cup frozen peas, thawed
3 eggs, beaten
1 teaspoon tomato paste
2 tablespoons lime juice
¼ teaspoon Tabasco sauce
1½ pounds cooked white rice,
   cooled (equivalent to
   ½ pound raw weight)
⅔ cup cashews, roughly chopped
2 tablespoons chopped
   fresh cilantro
salt and pepper

1 Heat the oil in a large non-stick
frying pan or wok and cook the shallots
until very crisp and golden. Remove
with a slotted spoon and drain on
paper towels.

2 Add the garlic and chili and cook
for 1 minute. Add the scallions and
pepper and cook for 3–4 minutes or
until beginning to soften.

3 Add the cabbage, cucumber and
peas and cook for 2 more minutes.

cilantro

scallions

red chili

cucumber

Tabasco sauce

white cabbage

garlic

red bell pepper

oil

cooked rice

eggs

peas

lime

shallots

cashews

tomato paste

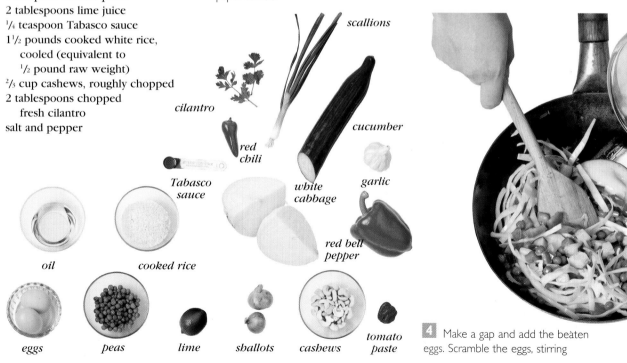

4 Make a gap and add the beaten
eggs. Scramble the eggs, stirring
occasionally, and then stir them into
the vegetables.

5 Add the tomato paste, lime juice and Tabasco and stir to combine.

6 Increase the heat and add the rice, cashews and cilantro with plenty of seasoning. Stir-fry for 3–4 minutes, until piping hot. Serve garnished with the crisp shallots and extra fresh cilantro, if desired.

Leek, Mushroom and Lemon Risotto

A delicious risotto, packed full of flavor, this is a great recipe for an informal supper with friends.

Serves 4

INGREDIENTS
1/2 pound trimmed leeks
generous 3 cups
    brown-cap mushrooms
2 tablespoons olive oil
3 garlic cloves, crushed
6 tablespoons butter
1 large onion, roughly chopped
scant 1³/₄ cups risotto (arborio) rice
5 cups hot vegetable stock
grated rind and juice of 1 lemon
²/₃ cup Parmesan cheese, freshly
    grated
¼ cup mixed chopped fresh chives
    and flat leaf parsley
salt and pepper
lemon wedges, to serve

leeks
vegetable stock
Parmesan cheese
lemon
butter
risotto rice
onion
garlic
brown-cap mushrooms
olive oil
parsley
chives

1 Wash the leeks well. Slice in half lengthwise and roughly chop. Wipe the mushrooms with paper towels and roughly chop.

2 Heat the oil in a large saucepan and cook the garlic for 1 minute. Add the leeks, mushrooms and plenty of seasoning and cook over medium heat for about 10 minutes or until softened and browned. Remove from the pan and set aside.

3 Add 1 ounce of the butter to the pan and cook the onion over medium heat for about 5 minutes, until softened and golden.

4 Stir in the rice and cook for 1 minute, until the grains begin to look translucent and are coated in the fat. Add a ladleful of stock to the pan and cook gently, stirring occasionally, until the liquid is absorbed.

5 Stir in more liquid as each ladleful is absorbed; this should take 20–25 minutes. The risotto will turn thick and creamy and the rice should be tender but not sticky.

6 Just before serving, stir in the leeks, mushrooms, remaining butter, grated lemon rind and 3 tablespoons of the juice, half the Parmesan and herbs. Adjust the seasoning and serve, sprinkled with the remaining Parmesan and herbs. Serve with lemon wedges.

Ratatouille Couscous

A rich mixture of zucchini, eggplant, peppers and tomatoes on a light, lemony couscous. Serve plenty of grated cheese to melt on the ratatouille.

Serves 6

INGREDIENTS
2 tablespoons olive oil
1 onion, roughly chopped
2 garlic cloves, crushed
1 red bell pepper, seeded and
    roughly chopped
3/4 pound zucchini, thickly sliced
10 ounces eggplant,
    roughly chopped
1 pound plum tomatoes,
    roughly chopped
2 tablespoons sun-dried tomato paste
1/4 cup mixed chopped fresh basil,
    parsley and thyme
salt and pepper

FOR THE COUSCOUS
2 1/4 cups hot vegetable stock
pinch of saffron strands
scant 1 3/4 cups couscous
grated rind and juice of 1 lemon
1/4 cup olive oil
3 tablespoons chopped fresh parsley
6 ounces Cheddar cheese, grated

1 Heat the oil in a large saucepan and cook the onion and garlic for 5 minutes, until beginning to soften but not color.

2 Add the pepper, zucchini and eggplant and stir-fry over medium heat for 5 minutes.

3 Add the tomatoes, tomato paste, mixed herbs and plenty of seasoning. Cover and cook over medium heat for about 20 minutes or until tender, thick and juicy. Simmer, uncovered, for a few minutes if the mixture is too wet.

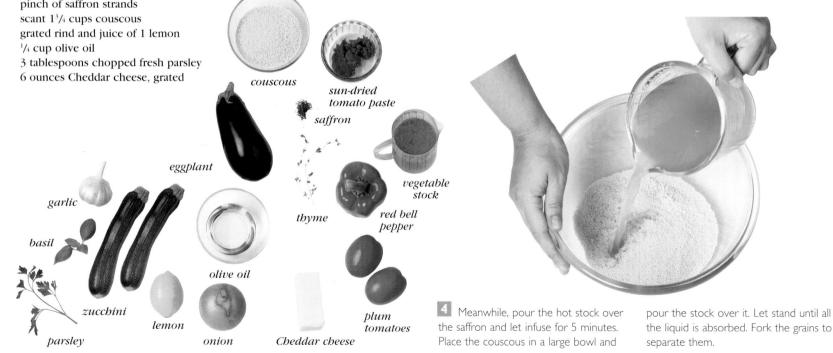

couscous

sun-dried
tomato paste

saffron

vegetable
stock

eggplant

thyme

red bell
pepper

garlic

basil

olive oil

zucchini

lemon

onion

Cheddar cheese

plum
tomatoes

parsley

4 Meanwhile, pour the hot stock over the saffron and let infuse for 5 minutes. Place the couscous in a large bowl and pour the stock over it. Let stand until all the liquid is absorbed. Fork the grains to separate them.

5 Whisk together the grated rind and juice of the lemon, olive oil, parsley and plenty of seasoning. Pour it over the couscous and stir in with a fork until combined. Transfer to a serving dish.

6 Adjust the ratatouille seasoning. Spoon it over the couscous and sprinkle with the grated cheese to serve.

Peanut Noodles

Add any of your favorite vegetables to this recipe, which is quick to make for a great mid-week supper – and increase the chili, if you can take the heat!

Serves 4

INGREDIENTS
1/2 pound medium egg noodles
2 tablespoons olive oil
2 garlic cloves, crushed
1 large onion, roughly chopped
1 red bell pepper, seeded and
    roughly chopped
1 yellow bell pepper, seeded and
    roughly chopped
3/4 pound zucchini, roughly chopped
generous 3/4 cup
    roasted unsalted peanuts,
    roughly chopped

FOR THE DRESSING
1/4 cup good-quality olive oil
grated rind and juice of 1 lemon
1 red chili, seeded and
    finely chopped
3 tablespoons chopped fresh chives
1–2 tablespoons balsamic vinegar
salt and pepper
chopped fresh chives, to garnish

red bell
pepper

garlic

balsamic
vinegar

red
chili

zucchini

peanuts

chives

onion

yellow bell pepper

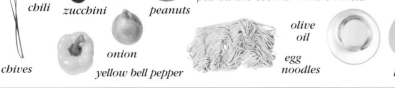
egg
noodles

olive
oil

lemon

1 Soak the noodles according to the package instructions and drain well.

2 Meanwhile, heat the oil in a very large frying pan or wok and cook the garlic and onion for 3 minutes or until beginning to soften. Add the peppers and zucchini and cook for 15 more minutes over medium heat, until beginning to soften and brown. Add the peanuts and cook for 1 more minute.

3 Whisk together the olive oil, grated rind and 3 tablespoons lemon juice, the chili, chives, plenty of seasoning and balsamic vinegar to taste.

4 Toss the noodles into the vegetables and stir-fry to heat through. Add the dressing, stir to coat and serve immediately, garnished with chopped fresh chives.

Potato, Parsnip and Cumin Tortilla

Three great flavors come together. Use a good aged Cheddar to balance them.

Serves 4-6

INGREDIENTS
¼ cup olive oil
1¼ pounds potatoes, thinly sliced
½ pound parsnips, thinly sliced
10 ounces onions, halved and
    thinly sliced
4 eggs, beaten
2 teaspoons cumin seeds
1 cup aged Cheddar cheese, grated
salt and pepper
fresh flat leaf parsley, to garnish

cumin seeds

parsnips

onions

potatoes

Cheddar cheese

eggs

parsley

olive oil

1 Heat 2 tablespoons of the oil in a frying pan, preferably non-stick, about 8 inches in diameter. Fry the potatoes, parsnips and onions for 2–3 minutes, turning occasionally; the pan will be quite full. Cover tightly and cook over gentle heat for about 30 minutes, turning occasionally, until softened and slightly golden.

2 Place the beaten eggs in a bowl, with the cumin, cheese and plenty of seasoning. Stir in the potatoes, parsnips and onions, until coated, being careful not to break up the potatoes.

3 Heat 2 tablespoons olive oil in the pan and add the potato mixture. Cook over low heat, until the egg begins to set. Use a spatula to prevent the tortilla from sticking to the sides of the pan.

4 Preheat the broiler to hot. When the base has set, after about 5 minutes, cover the pan handle with foil, and place under the broiler, until set and golden. Turn out and cut into wedges to serve, garnished with flat leaf parsley.

Spiced Tofu Stir-fry

You could add any quickly cooked vegetable to this stir-fry – try snow peas, sugar snap peas, leeks or thin slices of carrot.

Serves 4

INGREDIENTS
2 teaspoons ground cumin
1 tablespoon paprika
1 teaspoon ground ginger
good pinch of cayenne pepper
1 tablespoon superfine sugar
10 ounces tofu (bean curd)
¼ cup oil
2 garlic cloves, crushed
1 bunch scallions, sliced
1 red bell pepper, seeded and sliced
1 yellow bell pepper, seeded and sliced
generous 3 cups brown-cap
    mushrooms, halved or
    quartered, if necessary
1 large zucchini, sliced
¼ pound green beans, halved
scant ½ cup pine nuts
1 tablespoon lime juice
1 tablespoon clear honey
salt and pepper

red bell pepper
tofu
paprika
pine nuts
cayenne pepper
scallions *ground cumin* *clear honey* *oil*
ground ginger   *lime*
garlic
fine green beans   *zucchini*
yellow bell pepper *superfine sugar* *brown-cap mushrooms*

1 Combine the cumin, paprika, ginger, cayenne and sugar with plenty of seasoning. Cut the tofu into cubes and coat them in the spice mixture.

2 Heat some oil in a wok or large frying pan. Cook the tofu over high heat for 3–4 minutes, turning occasionally (be careful not to break up the tofu too much). Remove with a slotted spoon. Wipe out the pan with paper towels.

3 Add a little more oil to the pan and cook the garlic and scallions for 3 minutes. Add the remaining vegetables and cook over medium heat for 6 minutes or until beginning to soften and turn golden. Season well.

4 Return the tofu to the pan with the pine nuts, lime juice and honey. Heat through and serve immediately.

Oven-baked Vegetables with Cheese and Olives

Finishing the vegetables in the oven really brings out their natural flavors. Why not try adding fennel, carrot or mushrooms?

Serves 6

INGREDIENTS

4 small onions, about 1 pound
   total weight
2 red bell peppers, seeded
2 yellow bell peppers, seeded
10 ounces eggplant
1 pound zucchini
2 pounds butternut squash
   or pumpkin
olive oil
8 whole garlic cloves, unpeeled
2 tablespoons balsamic vinegar
24 black olives, pitted
½ pound Roquefort or other blue
   cheese, sliced
salt and freshly ground black pepper
crusty bread, to serve

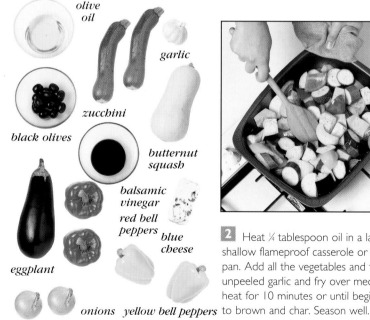

olive oil

garlic

zucchini

black olives

butternut squash

balsamic vinegar

red bell peppers

blue cheese

eggplant

onions   yellow bell peppers

1 Preheat the oven to 425°F. Peel and quarter the onions. Roughly chop the peppers, eggplant and zucchini into uniform pieces. Peel the butternut squash, remove the seeds and roughly chop the flesh.

2 Heat ¼ tablespoon oil in a large, shallow flameproof casserole or roasting pan. Add all the vegetables and the unpeeled garlic and fry over medium heat for 10 minutes or until beginning to brown and char. Season well.

3 Place the vegetables in the oven, uncovered, and cook, stirring occasionally, for 50 minutes or until tender and well browned. Stir in the balsamic vinegar, with 2 tablespoons of olive oil and plenty of seasoning.

4 Stir in the olives and lay the slices of cheese over the vegetables. Return to the oven for 5 minutes, until the cheese begins to melt. Serve with plenty of crusty bread to mop up the juices.

INDEX